NOTHING

&

EVERYTHING

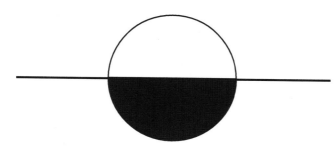

How to Stop Fearing Nihilism and Embrace the Void

Val N. Tine

This book is a gift – share it as you like

ISBN: 9781521711910

val.n.tine@protonmail.com

If you would like to read this without paying, distribute it more widely or even republish it, you can find the files at either of the following links:

https://www.dropbox.com/sh/gthoseohmhfkkrb/ AAAWmXJ9OLpVZ4pZnX9HBL41a?dl=0

https://tinyurl.com/scubeqt

NOTHING

&

EVERYTHING

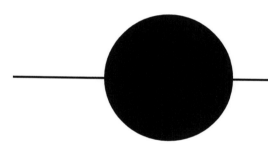

"Row row row your boat,

Gently down the stream,

Merrily merrily merrily merrily

Life is but a dream."

Nursery Rhyme

Do you ever ask yourself, as you try and fail to fall asleep at night, whether there is any meaning to your life? Do you ever struggle to get up in the morning, unable to see a reason to face another day? Do you ever despair that your life is insignificant, an unimportant fragment of a world that doesn't care? Do you ever suspect that this might all just be a dream or simulation, that this existence is fundamentally unreal in some sense? Do you ever question how it's possible for us to know anything, suspecting that our hard-won truths are mere illusion? Do you ever think suddenly that a moral dilemma is meaningless, that only prejudice and unexamined assumptions separate its sides? Do you ever doubt the existence of your self?

You are right to doubt. You have been told comforting stories about goodness and justice and truth that supposedly put these worries to rest, that give you a firm foundation on which to stand. Yet all those lessons you learnt don't seem to be adding up. Something is wrong, deeply wrong. Something important. You feel the ground beginning to shift beneath your feet.

Do you ever think that 'nothing is true and everything is permitted'?

2

This book could likely be distilled into those 7 words.

The first part of this book is about value, about the 'good and bad' and the 'good and evil' which we use to guide our actions. Yet, for all our moralizing, we can never get true judgements about what is good or bad or evil. The only guidance we receive is from ourselves, or from the beliefs of the society in which we live. So everything is permitted.

The second part of this book is about reason, about the 'true and false' and 'reason and logic' we use to impose some order upon this world. Yet we can never know whether our statements correspond to some objective reality, can never seem to get a straight answer from the reason we use to reach truth. So nothing is true.

"But if nothing is true, how can it be true that 'nothing is true and everything is permitted'?" This is a good question, one which will be answered eventually, once we have the words to explain it.

This book denies that we can have knowledge of either value or the world, and argues that talk of objective morality or reality is wrong. It argues for nihilism. This is a label that I happily apply, though there are other labels that could apply just as well – existentialism, absurdism, skepticism, sophistry, ironism, solipsism, egoism, subjectivism and so on. 'Nihilism' says it best though, with the least intellectual baggage. Just remember that the content of these pages is more important than the choice of word used to neatly label them. You can agree with one and not the other.

'Nihilism' does still have some baggage though, so let's be clear: this is not the nihilism of despair and sadness, nor depression and apathy, nor angsty teenage poetry. No, this nihilism is a joyous celebration. The reasons for this joy will become evident as we proceed through the book.

Many of you reading this will already believe some of it, on some level. If you are one of those readers, then please read these pages especially carefully. After all, the most dangerous books are the ones we vaguely agree with already, but which articulate our intuitions with a clarity we lack. When reading such a book a single lucid flash, the profound moment where you recognize your half-formed thoughts in the clear prose of another's hand, is often all it takes to reflexively agree with everything said afterwards. So be careful. I do not want your faith.

3

The ideas in this book aren't new, nor are they unique, nor are many of them even particularly original. They have been said thousands of times in different ways through the centuries. What I hope to do here is to say them in a way that is focused, understandable, and consistent. The best ideas are useless if they're buried in a haystack of irrelevant ones, or if they're expressed in words that no-one without an exclusive and expensive university education can understand, or if the person writing them lacks the resolve to follow them through to their conclusion.

Apologies to those whose ideas I have used and abused and who I have not named but, ultimately, the content of an idea is more important than who happened to say it. All of this would be just as meaningful if it were murmured by you drunkenly in your sleep, or spelt out in seashells washed ashore by the waves.

4

You've lying awake in the middle of the night, unable to sleep. You hear a noise and dismiss it. You try to sleep again and, just as you're drifting off, you hear it again, louder. You get out of bed. It's pitch black, and no-one else is in the house. A shiver runs down your spine as you flick the light switch. It doesn't turn on. You hear the noise again, louder still.

You keep trying the switch, or fumble around for matches, anything to regain illumination.

Or you freeze, paralyzed, unable to move.

Or, when there is no light, you summon the strength to walk through the darkness.

GOOD
&
BAD

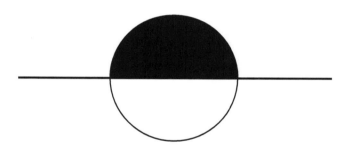

"Whatever is done out of love takes place beyond good
and evil"

Friedrich Nietzsche, Beyond Good and Evil

5

What is the good life? What is the right thing to do? What would a just society look like? How should I act? What is the meaning of life? Many consider answering such questions to be the great task of philosophy, of society, perhaps of existence itself. Answers are discovered by the sharpest thinkers, championed by the most righteous activists, upheld by the greatest leaders, then killed and died for by the most forgotten millions.

Asking these questions has been a terrible, millennia-long mistake.

6

Some try to answer. They claim that they have discovered what is good and bad and evil in the same way that we have mapped out the orbits of the planets in the night sky. They say they have found something that *is* right, or just, or noble, and that with this compass our lives can be guided towards the good. What they assume here is that there are right values to have – that placing value on one thing, action, or state over another can be correct or incorrect in the same way that your answer to a math problem could be. This is wrong. The moralists have found only illusion.

But even when we recognize this, understanding that there is no right nor good nor justice, those questions still bewitch us. They imply that an answer is necessary, that without one our lives are meaningless, that absent a compass we will be forever lost. So we become convinced that we need a reason to value things and, when that reason disappears, so does that value. We fall into despair, thinking that it is all just meaningless noise, perhaps dedicating ourselves to cruel self-interest or fleeting pleasures. A light inside of us slowly dies. This is unnecessary.

It is not possible to answer these questions. But neither is it necessary. We can live our lives knowing in our hearts what we value, without asking our minds whether we are 'right' or 'correct' or 'justified' in doing so. So stop asking 'what is the meaning of life?'

No answer is coming.

8

What do we mean by 'values'? Values concern your preferences in this world. You might value apples over oranges, honesty over lying, capitalism over communism, living peacefully over violently, the person you love over anyone else in the world and so on. Everyone has values – without them we would have no cause to do anything at all. We all want some things over others. We would all do some things but not others. We would all like the world to be one way over another.

We can value things in different ways though.

You might believe your values to be *objective*. You might value honesty over lying and believe that honesty just *is* better. That it doesn't matter what some people *think* is better, but that there is something inherently better about honesty than lies. Something that makes lying bad no matter whether people actually value truth or not. If you were to value honesty like this, then people who didn't share this value, liars for example, would be not only different but *wrong*. When a value is held to be objective like this, we'll call it a judgement (and maybe also a justified value, or an objective value). Valuing something objectively will be called judging it. And coming up with reasons why a value is true will be called justifying that value.

Or you might believe your values to be *subjective*. You might prefer apples over oranges (or honesty over lies, or

9

peace over war, or capitalism over communism) without thinking that there's anything inherently better about apples. You might just think of it as something that comes down to taste, a difference more about the people doing the valuing than the things being valued. If you were to value apples like this, people who liked oranges better wouldn't be incorrect – they'd just have a different taste to you. When a value is held like this, we'll call it a choice (or a chosen value, or a subjective value). Valuing something while recognizing the subjectivity of that value will be called choosing it.

The way I'm using these words might not quite align with how you use them. You might mean something completely different by 'value', or 'judgement', or 'choice'. That difference might then lead you to think that my arguments about why judgements are always wrong are nonsensical, or that when I argue for choices I'm actually arguing for objectively held values. That's why I've explained what I mean by these words in this context – so we won't be held up by the fact that one word can have different meanings.

9

You might object that this meaning of 'judgement' is extremely wide, and you would be right. Judgements are everywhere. They are there when the moralizer says that some actions are moral and others immoral. They are there when the critic holds one painting to be sublime and another uninspired. They are there when the politician claims that their econo-political system is superior to the enemy's. They are there when the philosopher declares that they have found the good life. They are there when the activist denounces the violation of rights. They are there when your parents tell you to get a 'good' job. They are there when the prophet brings their commandments down from the mountain. And in both the slurs of the racist, the wounds of the martyr, the kindness of the cruel and the cruelty of the kind, they are there.

10

That claim to objectivity is crucial for how people actually think about and use judgements. It isn't an incidental part that can be discarded without consequence.

Because judgements are objective in some way, then philosophers and various other academics can find the right one by thinking about them. This means we can have debates about what the good life is, departments of universities set up to study ethics and so on.

Because there is one right answer, some judgements can be correct and others incorrect. Instead of just acknowledging the fact that others may value differently, a judgement allows you to say that those other people's values are wrong and that your own are right, and allows you to decide between numerous competing values.

Because that right answer is something outside the individual, this objectivity allows you to think of yourself as being guided by values, following the judgements laid out for you in advance. This leads to a certainty that eliminates your responsibility of having to choose, and a sense of obligation to act in certain ways.

Because the right answer is something beyond the individual or society, it makes you feel that you're serving something much greater than yourself. If morality, justice, and value are somehow written into the universe itself, then to act in harmony with them is to take part in some sort of universal meaning. This gives you a deeper purpose to your life.

Because the right answer is a fact, a statement which can be true or false, you can place it into a broader logical structure. The reason why one thing is good could be applied to other things. Knowing that one action is moral would allow you to infer the morality of actions like it. Knowing that one system is just could imply that contradictory systems are unjust. You could even look at a broad range of things considered 'good' and infer a general rule of 'goodness' connecting them. These inferences allow judgments to be woven together into broader moral systems.

11

Further, where you have judgements you will usually find ideas of obligation, and morality. These are the ideas that you *should* or *ought* or *must* do something, that something is *morally* required of you. These stand or fall together with judgements more generally – if judgements don't make sense, if things aren't objectively better than each other, then obligation and morality don't make any sense either.

This is the case regardless of the specific way you think about morality. If you think it consists of following the right rules (deontology), then your system is undermined if no rule is better than any other. If you think it consists of getting the right outcomes (utilitarianism), then your system is undermined if no outcome is better than any other. If you think it consists of acting as a good person would (virtue ethics), then your system is undermined if no person is better than any other. If nothing *is* good or bad then nothing is right or wrong, good or evil, just or unjust, moral or immoral.

14

The main point of the next 8,000 or so words is that values can never be justified – we can never know whether something is better than another thing, and it's likely that no quality of goodness exists. So if you care about truth (and we'll return to that 'if', and that 'truth' later) then judgements can't be made. That means that things like ethics and morality have to be thrown out as well. It also means that the implications of objectivity that were explained in §10 disappear. That is the first half of this first book.

But we're also concerned with what fills the void that's left. Do you try to surreptitiously bring judgements back in again? Do you collapse, unable to even get out of bed? Do you devote your life to material gain, sensual pleasure and/or endless distraction? I will try to show that these are not the only options, that there are ways of choosing the values you would like to live by without first cloaking them in an objectivity they'll never have. Values were always subjective, after all. All it takes is to experience and embrace them as such.

So what is wrong with judgements? Why is their claim to objectivity never justified? Why can't one thing be better than another? We'll go through 3 reasons:

REGRESSION

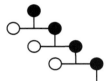

13

The first reason is the regress.

The regress attacks our ability to justify values into judgements. The reasons for this are simple. Every belief has to be justified by something. Otherwise we wouldn't have any reason to believe it. That justification usually comes in the form of other beliefs that entail our first belief, but those other beliefs need to be justified as well, usually by yet more beliefs, and so on. Further, a judgement about what is good or bad can't be justified by just any belief – it needs to be justified by another judgement.

14

Imagine that you've just run over your housemate Sally's cat. You're tempted to pin the blame on your other housemate Jack though, as he hasn't done the dishes in a while and is always late paying rent. You want to know what to do. You think that 'It would be morally wrong to tell Sally that Jack ran over her cat'. But you don't want to take that judgement for granted. You want to make sure that you've got this one right (and may be looking for any excuse to get Jack out of the house).

So you need an argument that justifies why you shouldn't lie to Sally. And imagine you come up with this:

Lying is mean

Telling Sally that Jack ran over her cat would be lying

Therefore, it would be morally wrong to tell Sally that Jack ran over her cat

You realize you've made a mistake here though. All you've really proven is that telling Sally that Jack ran over her cat would be mean. You haven't yet shown why it would be morally wrong, or worse, or bad. All you have is a factual description. This is because getting a conclusion that something is morally wrong requires you to have a reason why it is morally wrong. If your only reasons are describing the facts, they can't justify a conclusion about whether those facts are good or bad. To justify that sort of conclusion, the first line has to be changed:

Lying is morally wrong

Telling Sally that Jack ran over her cat would be lying

Therefore, it would be morally wrong to tell Sally that Jack ran over her cat

This argument is valid. If both of the first two lines are true, then the third line has to be true too. But to get to that point we needed a reason that concerned itself with when something was morally right or wrong.

This is a practical example of the is/ought distinction – you can't justify a conclusion about what *ought* to be from reasons that only tell you what *is*.

But, coming back to our dilemma, the first two lines in that argument might not be true after all. And if they aren't true then the conclusion won't have been justified. The argument would be unsound. Now here it's pretty obvious that the second line is true – you ran over the cat after all, not Jack. But you want to investigate the 'Lying is morally wrong' reason. So you come up with some premises justifying it:

Breaking others' trust is morally wrong

Lying breaks others' trust

Therefore, Lying is morally wrong

Again, this seems pretty valid. But you get to the same problem again – how do you know that breaking others' trust is morally wrong? How do you justify that judgement?

If you try to justify it, that requires another judgement as a reason, and you're back in the same position as before. But if you don't justify it, then 'lying is morally wrong' hasn't been justified at all. And if 'lying is morally wrong' isn't justified, then 'It would be morally wrong to tell Sally that Jack ran over her cat' isn't justified either, and you don't have a solution to your moral dilemma. You can't let this chain go on infinitely either, as you certainly don't get an answer then. Nor can you let the chain loop back on itself – e.g. 'breaking the trust of others must be morally wrong, because otherwise I'd be able to do the morally reprehensible act of lying to Sally about who ran over the dog'. That would be circular, which doesn't prove anything.

15

But you may not be satisfied with this. 'But everyone thinks that breaking others' trust is wrong! Surely that's a good enough reason!'. Let's see:

Breaking others' trust is thought to be morally wrong

Lying breaks others' trust

Therefore, Lying is thought to be morally wrong

No. Again, all you get out of this is the conclusion that lying is *thought to be morally wrong*, not that it *is*. You get a statement about what people *believe* to be true, not what *is* true. We already know that lots of people think that lying is morally wrong. That they thought so was never in doubt. But what we wanted to know was whether were right to think so, whether that belief reflected something besides itself. A judgement holds itself as objective after all – about what *is* true. And without that perceived objectivity, as you'll recall, the reasons why you'd seek to make judgements disappear.

But you're still unsatisfied. You grasp for some other reasons besides social consensus. 'But breaking others' trust defies God's will! It causes pain! It breaks the social contract! It just feels wrong!' And, in your defence, any of those may be true. But all they prove is that:

Breaking others' trust (defies God's will/causes pain/breaks the social contract/feels wrong)

Lying breaks others' trust

Therefore, lying (defies God's will/causes pain/breaks the social contract/feels wrong)

None of these statements about breaking others' trust break through from fact into judgement, so they too can only be used to justify yet more factual statements. To justify a judgement you would need a further premise, a premise which establishes that something that defies God's will/causes pain/breaks the social contract/feels wrong *is* morally wrong. And that would be a judgement that you'd need to justify further, and the cycle would begin again.

16

But maybe you fall back from this, and declare that there are some judgements that are just self-evident. That are so obvious they need no justification at all. Something like 'murdering a child is wrong', or, 'life, liberty, and the pursuit of happiness are good'.

What do you really mean by 'self-evident' here though? Do you just mean that you and everyone you can imagine would agree with you? Because, if so, you've still shown nothing. That would prove that everyone thought those judgements were correct, but goes nowhere in proving that they *are* correct. Feeling something strongly enough does not make the world bend around your feelings (though we will return to what we might mean by 'the world' a bit later on).

Or maybe you contest that there is such a strict distinction between is and ought. Don't we imply that something we call 'mean' is also morally wrong? And aren't statements about what is good or bad informed by what we believe to be true or false? Yes, but no.

Maybe, in ordinary language, we would assume that something called 'mean' is implied to be morally wrong. But that automatic assessment, that jump from 'mean' to 'morally wrong' is precisely what we're trying to interrogate here, and what needs to be held up to scrutiny. And while people's views of what the facts *are* obviously influence their thoughts about whether something is good or not, that's mainly because different judgements apply to different factual situations, not because there is no difference between facts and value. For example, whether someone is aware that *you* ran over Sally's cat will probably influence whether they think it's morally correct for you to tell Sally that Jack ran over the cat. But that's because it changes their assessment of whether you, right now, are lying, not whether lying in general is permissible. These are separate questions.

17

So judgement a has to be justified by judgement b, judgement b by judgement c, c by d and so on. But the final link in that chain can never itself be justified. And if d isn't justified then neither is c, and if not c then not b either, and if not b then, well, not a. The whole structure collapses like a house of cards.

RELATIVISM

● ○

The second reason is relativism.

Relativism is about the variations in judgements across time and space. That variation is plain to see. For some, pain is to be avoided above all else, but for others its pleasure that should be eschewed. For some glory, for others humility. For some liberty, for others obedience. Some people like the values society has now, some would prefer to change things further, and others would like to take us back a few hundred years or so. There are huge differences in what people view as valuable, what they hold to be good, what they think is moral, differences that can't just be explained by them holding different views about the facts of the world.

There is also variation across time. What was judged to be good and moral in one society changes dramatically, such that what was considered a great good can come to be considered a great wrong. Take slavery – for a long period many people considered it to be the natural and right order of things, but it is now regarded as a terrible historical atrocity. Extending that into the future, there are future societies that will almost certainly view many things that we are doing now as fundamentally wrong. Industrial agriculture and environmental degradation are likely cases of this, as is perhaps the modern slavery of US prison labor.

Further, many of these different judgements are contradictory. If you think that the good life is one of hedonistic pleasure, and I think that it is one of stoic reserve, then our judgements contradict one another. But, as judgements, these beliefs are claiming to both describe an objective reality. And it can't be the case that the good life is both objectively stoic and hedonistic, because the truth of one means the falsehood of the other. So we cannot both be right.

Each judgement is a tiny minority, surrounded by the thousands of conflicting judgements held right now. And those judgements held right now are an even tinier fraction of all the judgements that have been held in the past, or will be held in the future. And all of the people who hold, have held, or will hold those judgements all believe that they are in the right. Further, many of these judgements are contradictory – in which case only one of that contradictory set can be true.

A few conclusions come from this:

19

Firstly, what are the odds that any one of your judgements are the correct ones? That you have somehow stumbled upon even one correct answer? That those countless billions in the past, present and future who disagree with you are wrong?

Given the amount of judgements, and that only one can be correct in cases of contradiction, any individual judgement has only an infinitesimal chance of being true.

You may think that your particular judgements are better justified than the others – that you have well-founded reasons for thinking that all the others are in the wrong. But remember that everyone who you disagree with also believes that they are definitely in the right, and presumably have their own seemingly unshakeable reasons. So a feeling that you are well justified in your beliefs shouldn't give you any relief – everyone has that feeling. Yet the difference remains.

Probabilistically, relativism means that any one judgement has only a tiny chance of being correct. This doesn't mean that it cannot be true, of course. But to have confidence under these conditions would require strong evidence, evidence that never seems to appear.

20

Secondly, relativism makes it highly unlikely that we can rely on our perceptions of what is good and bad. You may think that we can do exactly that – that when you judge something as good or bad you're perceiving or intuiting that objective goodness or badness in a similar sort of way to your perception of these words in front of you. If you could perceive qualities of goodness and badness like that, then you might have some sort of a foundation from which to build a system of true judgements, and so escape the regress raised earlier.

But relativism undermines this. The public shaming of a young unmarried couple for adultery would be perceived as a terrible wrong by you, I assume. But there are many who would see such a scene as morally necessary, as a triumph of public morality over private decadence. If there is a right answer at all, one of you has to be wrong. But there is no way of telling which one of you is wrong without referring to something beyond those clashing perceptions, to something objective that could function as a tie-breaker. But we only brought perception in because we lack that 'something beyond', and need, as a fallback, to find some basis in perception for our judgements. Perceiving the right judgement is not an answer to the regress, because deciding between clashing perceptions would require exactly the kind of knowledge that the regress rules out.

It is true, of course, that people sometimes perceive incorrectly. For example, you might mistake long grass for a lurking tiger. But when people perceive incorrectly they can generally be made to see the error of their ways by looking again. If I show you the grass again you will realize it is no tiger. Yet differences in how goodness or badness are perceived are not like that – they are too persistent, too durable, and are not resolved by simply looking again. That leaves us again with the question of who is perceiving correctly, a question to which we still have no answer.

21

Thirdly, relativism makes it impossible for law or social consensus to ground morality. You might, like many others, try to use these institutions as guides to your judgement. If law or social consensus disapprove then surely, you might reason, that is because those institutions reflect a deeper objective truth.

Yet these institutions change over time and space. There are many different legal orders and many different societies, each with their own consensus and judgements. Again, many of these conflict. Which of these judgements is right? To answer this you would need to already have something to assist you in deciding that question, something to choose between these competing claims. But you appealed to law or social consensus precisely because you didn't have anything to do that with. Law or social consensus could perhaps be reliable guides, but only for those who didn't need a guide in the first place.

Law and social consensus also change over time. Imagine that you believe in taking judgements from social consensus. So the most popular judgement will be the correct one. But social consensus changes. So every majority judgement today (making it true) was held only by a minority (making it false) at one point in time. By that logic, a judgement that was false 20 years ago becomes true now. But if that belief was false then, how has it since become true? If judgements really do describe an objective truth, you wouldn't expect that objective truth to be quite so malleable, nor so suspiciously attuned to changes in public opinion and legislation.

22

Fourthly, this relativism means that we can't test our judgements about what is good and bad. If you wanted to sort fresh apples from rotten apples, for instance, you could test the different ways of doing so. You could sort them by hand and sight, by some sort of machine, by chemical analysis etc. You wouldn't have to settle for trying to figure out which method would be better in advance, either. You could just see which method sorted the apples best. This is because there is agreement on the difference between fresh and rotten apples. You can test hypotheses about the best apple sorting techniques by subjecting them to experiments.

You cannot apply the same method to judgements though. This is because the question is how to tell what's fresh from what's rotten. If you don't know what good and bad are, you can't experiment to find the best method for telling them apart.

23

So relativism makes it highly unlikely that any one judgement is true. Which raises the standard of proof you'd probably need to be convinced of any one judgement. It then eliminates the possibility of using perception, law, social consensus, or experiment to try to reach that standard.

INFLUENCE

24

The third reason is influence.

Even if coming to a correct judgement were possible in an abstractly rational kind of way, we humans aren't entirely abstract rational creatures. We are also influenced by many non-rational factors – by the society we live in, our position within it, by our biology, by the weather and so on. And, just as these factors influence us in general, they influence us in what we judge to be good and bad.

25

This influence over judgements is undeniable. Take the influence of society. You can see that there is greater similarity between the moral judgements of people within the same country than there is between people of different countries. If you're a citizen of Saudi Arabia, your judgements are likely to be closer to a fellow Saudi Arabian's than to a Norwegian's. There will of course be outliers in both countries where this doesn't hold, but it's likely true in general.

But how do you explain that conformity? Maybe, people living in one society have relatively similar judgements because societies have a certain set of values that they influence people into holding. There are many ways in which this influence might operate – schools, media, churches, advertising, politicians, family, workplaces, peers, laws, literature and so on.

The same influence goes for your place within a particular society. A young person is more likely to have judgements in common with other young people than old people, and vice versa. So age probably has an influence on what judgements you make. And so on, with various other demographic factors like income, class, caste and so on.

This has two key implications.

26

Firstly, supposing that some judgements are correct, this influence can't only influence people towards those correct judgements.

There are many different societies after all, influencing people to make many different and contradictory judgements. And where those judgements are contradictory, only one of them can be correct. So, at least, the vast majority of this social pressure has to be pushing away from the right answer.

So how do you tell which of your judgements might be true in some way, and which are just the product of social conditioning? Can we tell by looking within ourselves? No. After all, almost everyone considers their own judgements to be a product of themselves, of their own thoughts, of their own inquiry. Yet the social influence on our judgements is undeniable. So, evidently, we can't trust introspection to give us accurate answers to this question.

Further, you can't just examine which one of your judgments you've actually put some thought in to. This is because that social influence also affects which arguments you will hear, which you will accept, what assumptions you will have and so on. It is embedded within you, not imposed from above. It is constitutive, not coercive.

So you know that many of your judgements are likely the result of social influence. But you don't have any way of telling which ones are. That ambiguity means you have to be suspicious of all of them, and provides a strong reason for believing none of them.

You could repeat this same analysis with a whole range of other potential influences: the judgements of your family as you were growing up, evolutionary hardwiring of certain likes and dislikes, your biological needs, the numerous cognitive biases you possess, your random first impressions of things and so on.

All of these are likely to influence what you view as good and bad. But you don't have a way of knowing where and when they do so. Even assuming the existence of true judgements, how are you going to find them through this interference? How are you going to isolate the signal in all this noise? Any judgement you come to is likely to be result of any number of external factors instead. In that context, why should you feel justified in any individual judgement?

27

There is a second implication though, about how we explain why people actually hold judgements. On the one hand we have these hypothetical attributes of objective 'goodness' and 'badness' which, if somehow decoded, will justify our values and lead us to true judgements. On the other, we have a huge number of factors that influence the judgements we actually make – society, biology, coincidence, personality etc.

Both of these are essentially trying to explain the same thing – why we feel that some things are objectively better than others. We will label these as two separate explanations.

Objectivity says that some things are better and some are worse, that we can figure out which are which, and that *that* leads us to feel that some things are objectively good etc. *Influence*, on the other hand, says that we feel that some things are objectively better because of the way society, biology, personality and various other factors shape us into doing so.

But, even if you believe that the *objectivity* explanation applies to your beliefs, you still have to believe the *influence* explanation for the beliefs of everyone else – otherwise you can't explain why the beliefs of other people cluster together in societies like they do, nor can you really account for everyone who disagrees with you. So the choice is this: you can choose the *objectivity* explanation for yourself and the *influence* explanation for everyone who disagrees, or the *influence* explanation for everyone.

Influence applying to everyone is much more plausible than *objectivity* applying to you and *influence* applying to everyone who disagrees. It requires only one explanation to be true, as opposed to both explanations being true, so is inherently more probable. It also doesn't require any strange exceptionalism whereby you and the people you agree with are exempt from the social and biological forces that condition everybody else. And, finally, it doesn't require people to be able to have same way of divining objective goodness and badness – something that is very unlikely for all the reasons already gone into.

28

Ultimately, we can explain why people believe the judgements they hold without invoking things like inherent goodness or objective morality, let alone strange abilities to perceive these qualities directly. Instead, we can explain things simply and plausibly by saying that people largely believe and feel these things under the influence of all sorts of biological, social, and personal factors. Doing so is much simpler, and makes far more sense.

But even if you want that *objectivity* explanation to operate in some cases, and the *influence* explanation to operate in others, you still need a way of telling those cases apart. Some independent and reliable method of assessing moral value, maybe, or a known list of true judgements that you could check against. Perhaps then we could finally know whether and when we were really accessing moral truth.

But such method does not exist. And such a list has never been found. So, at the very least, no individual judgement can be trusted. And at the end of the day, believing that some judgements are correct, but acknowledging that you'll never be able to know which ones are, isn't all that different in practice from abandoning judgements altogether. A morality that is merely hypothetical is no morality at all.

Q/A

● ○

○ ●

Q - But isn't it human nature to believe in good and bad? Don't people intrinsically believe that some things are good and evil?

A - Maybe. But if we did that still wouldn't answer the question. Even if we naturally believe that some things are good and some things are bad, it doesn't follow that those things we naturally believe in are true. It's probably natural for humans to believe in gods and spirits, but the naturalness of that belief doesn't make those spirits real. It's natural for us to believe things in line with the gambler's fallacy, but that doesn't mean that the roulette table really *is* any more likely to spin red after a run of black. So even if those claims about human nature were true, they go nowhere in proving that those naturally held values *are* objective or that those naturally held judgements *are* correct.

30

Q - Okay, maybe we can't have a single unquestionable judgement that can serve as a foundation for everything else. Sure. Maybe if we want justified values we have to accept that they'll be a little circular. Fine. But surely it's okay if we have beliefs that support each other, are coherent, and exist together in a sort of reflective equilibrium? If we can't accept that, how can we believe any judgements?'

A - 'No. This is because it's possible to imagine (and name) different moral systems that are all circular and self-supporting, but which come to contradictory conclusions about what is good and bad. Imagine on the one hand that you're someone with 21st century liberal/progressive views about what is good and just. That you have a pretty circular and self-supporting system of ideas and moral views that nonetheless lacks an unambiguous justification. And that you think that this gives you a right to call this set of beliefs true. So far so good.

But if this belief system is true then you can't have another belief system, that is also true, that contradicts it. And imagine on the other hand that you have a neo-Nazi, or an evangelical Christian, or a Buddhist monk, or a hardline anarcho-syndicalist. And that their belief systems are just as circular and mutually supportive as yours, but that they contradict yours in content at every point. If you call your belief system true because of that supportive circularity, then you have to admit that their belief systems are true as well. So you have numerous true belief systems that are radically inconsistent or, to put it in other way, you have numerous 'true' belief systems of which only one can actually be true. And we're back at the beginning again.

31

Q - Wait, this relativism nonsense doesn't hold at all. Surely everyone can agree on some basics, like 'don't harm others' or 'do onto others as you would have done to you'?

A - I don't think this is the case. Firstly, I doubt that any such agreement exists, especially when you include other cultures, the past, and the imagined future. It's only really possible to get agreement on basics when your survey of humanity is an extremely limited one.

Secondly, to get any hypothetical agreement you would have to state judgements at an extremely high level of generality, such that the process of inferring anything useful from them would just create disagreement at a different level. For example, you might be able to get people to agree on some sort of incredibly vague commandment like 'Do good'. But then you'd just get disagreement about what 'good' is, or what it might mean to 'do' something or not. Anything general enough to get you across-the-board agreement could never be specific enough to provide actual guidance.

32

Q - Of course we know when something is good. We call something good when it fulfils its purpose. A 'good' hammer is one that can smack nails in well. We just need to know the purpose of something, see whether it's doing it well, and if it is then it's good! Easy.

A - Perhaps that is true for one sense of the word 'good', but that meaning of 'good' isn't the same as the one that we're using here. A machine gun's purpose is to kill people, and we might call a machine gun that was really good at killing people a 'good' machine gun in a purpose-fulfilling sense. But we would still be able to say that this machine gun was 'bad' in an objective sense. We might even say that it was bad in an objective sense *because of* how well it fulfilled its human-killing purpose. All your point proves is that one word – 'good' – can have multiple meanings, and that it is easy to be led astray by puns.

Besides, purpose could never be a guide to the objective value of things, because purposes are assigned to things by humans. Nothing has a purpose in itself. It merely exists. A hammer without humanity is just a weird bit of wood and metal. So an examination of purpose tells us only about humanity, and doesn't lead us outside of ourselves to something objective, something that could be a guide between the different valuations that humans make and the different purposes that they assign.

Q - This is the sort of teenage, undergraduate nihilism that gets laughed out of 101 philosophy courses. You're wasting my time. Get a real philosophical position.

A - If you are in a 101 philosophy course or a philosophy department, and if you do bring up the ideas and contentions contained in this book, then you will indeed get laughed out of your class. There is a good reason for this. Such places are meant for exploration – earnestly learning about thinkers' ideas, engaging charitably with their key contentions, exploring the linkages between different philosophers, and cautiously contributing a modest refinement here and there. This book isn't useful for any of that work. In fact, it attempts to destroy the foundations upon which such work could be done. That doesn't mean that this book is wrong. But it means that this book is a complete waste of time from the viewpoint of academic philosophy.

However, we are not currently doing academic philosophy. And, outside that academic philosophy viewpoint, in which your particular criticism made sense, it instead sounds like the sort of dismissive, ad hominem attack of someone who's run out of real counter-arguments. If your 'real philosophical position' can't withstand even undergraduate criticism then perhaps it's you who are wasting your own time.

34

Q - Wait, but can't we just look at things that get called 'good', see what they have in common, then isolate that unifying principle? Then we'll be able to find other things that accord with that principle, which will also be good.

A - No. All that would tell us is what people *describe* as good. It wouldn't tell us what *is* good. It doesn't provide us with any mechanism for transcending what is held to be good in our particular social context, nor does it give us anything that would let us know that *this* conception of what is good is true, but that *that* conception is false. The absence of such a definitive answer is precisely what is causing us problems in the first place – different things are described as 'good' in many different languages and cultures.

35

Q - Wait, but what if 'good' doesn't really refer to anything objective at all? We would then have to determine what the word means from how it's used. From what I can see, 'Good' is just a short-hand term to make factual descriptions like generous, brave, or nice, and 'bad' is just a short-hand term to describe things like cruel, nasty, or selfish. All this talk about claims to objectivity is beside the point – the task is one of defining these words by how they're used.

A - This is highly misleading. Regardless of what specific qualities good and bad get used to describe (generous vs selfish etc.), they also get used in a way that implies that they are objective facts. Contradictory values get called wrong, we infer certain judgements from other judgements, we consider ourselves guided by judgements rather than creators of them, we think we can work them out rationally etc. They also get explicitly described as objective, e.g. 'We hold these truths to be self-evident, that all men are created equal, that they are endowed by their Creator with certain unalienable Rights, that among these are Life, Liberty and the pursuit of Happiness'. So 'good' and 'bad' clearly imply some sort of claim to objectivity. They aren't just shorthand for sets of things that *are* valued. They also imply that that value is an objective one.

So perhaps you could redefine this claim to objectivity out of these words. But then it would be *you* who wasn't defining them by their use, by ignoring the claim to objectivity underwriting their more specific applications.

However, if you feel like persisting, and if the only way you can defend 'good' and 'bad' is by redefining all objectivity from them, then go ahead. But be honest about what that redefinition involves sacrificing.

36

Q - Wait, but you haven't proved that statements about good and bad are *false* either. At most, all you've shown is that we can't have any knowledge of them, not that they definitively don't exist. So how can you know that 'everything is permitted'?

A - A truth which I can never encounter or experience is for all intents and purposes non-existent. An objective morality which can give me no guidance in life, as I can never know when my values align with it, is functionally the same as one that does not exist at all – in either event I must make my choices alone. This is not a philosophical treatise on the ontological status of moral judgements, but a practical book about how you relate to them and their absence. So being unable to disprove their existence is irrelevant.

37

Q - But what about a little thing called the social contract? We agree to give up a certain part of our freedom in exchange for safety. That's where we get moral obligations, and that's where we get the obligation to adhere to them.

A - No. Firstly, that social contract has never existed – none of us make an agreement with the state to sign away our freedom like that.

But even if we did, how would such an agreement create morally binding obligations? To do that, it would have to be immoral to break promises. And that moral principle would have to exist, and bind me, *before* I signed the social contract. Otherwise, breaking that agreement would have no weight. So the social contract can't actually be the total source of moral obligation as, logically, the obligation to keep promises needs to pre-exist it. So you need some justification for promise keeping that comes from a source outside the social contract. But you only appealed to the fiction of a 'social contract' because no such outside source could be found. And we're back at square one again.

38

Q - OK, so even if moral obligations and judgements are out, I definitely have my rights, right?

A - No. All of those rights to be treated or not treated in certain ways become meaningless if you remove the concepts of obligation and goodness. Saying that you have a right has to mean that others have a corresponding obligation towards you. 'I have a right to freedom of speech' would be meaningless without the implication that 'everyone else has an obligation not to interfere with my freedom of speech.' If, as I maintain, there's no such thing as obligation, then rights become meaningless. So rights (including property rights) cannot be substituted in as an alternative when morality and value fail.

39

Q - Even if you're right, aren't you concerned that this is a dead end for ethics? Isn't it more important to allow progression, to allow for further refinement and development, rather than just shutting it down? Isn't that the more constructive and mature thing to do?

A - Development to what end? So that we can develop a more elaborate and refined system of nonsense? An astrologer might make the same objection – that it would be a dead end in astrology to call out its absurdity, and that it would be more constructive to continue refining it instead. Such an objection may be convincing to another astrologer, a fellow sage who has spent their life reading the stars and cannot bear the thought that it was all for nothing. To them, it would undoubtedly be wiser to finesse the theory further, refining concepts and predictions, ignoring the gaping hole at the center to better make progress around the edges. To me, though, these sound like desperate excuses. Build that tower as high as you like, it will always be built on sand.

40

Q - But you can't possibly be right! After all, if we lived in a world without objective morality life wouldn't be worth living, and there wouldn't be anything to stop anyone from doing anything, and society would fall apart. So there must be objective value in the world!

A - This is wrong in many ways but, to be fair, also very common – the fact that one answer paints a nicer picture of reality gets used strangely often as a reason in favor of that nicer answer.

Nevertheless, the argument makes no sense.

First of all, it's circular. Perhaps you outline some consequences of goodness and morality not existing, or of people not believing that they exist. You then label those consequences as 'bad' or 'immoral' or 'unjust'. Then, from that badness, you infer that good and bad must really exist. But to get to that point you had to label those consequences as 'bad'. And labelling those consequences as 'bad' relies on the reality of goodness and badness. But the reality of goodness and badness was exactly the thing you were trying to prove here. So, to make this argument, you have to presuppose that goodness and badness exist in order to prove the existence of goodness and badness. This is circular, and it proves nothing.

Secondly, there's no logical connection between saying that something is or would be good and proving that it exists. *Ought* cannot be derived from *is*, as we discussed earlier, but neither can *is* be derived from *ought*. The fact that something would be good, or that things would be better if people believed in it, doesn't mean that that thing exists. You might think that world peace would be good, but that 'good' doesn't conjure world peace into existence. You might think that society would be better if everyone earnestly believed in Santa Clause, but that 'better' doesn't mean that an immortal bearded man *really* crawls down countless chimneys in a single night bearing gifts for virtuous children.

Thirdly, I would question your predictions of what a world without objective goodness, or a society without a belief in objective goodness, really looks like. I'm not going to say that such a world or society is *better* than the one we're currently in. But I don't think things would pan out quite the way that you expect. This will be dealt with later.

41

Q - Be that as it may, I still refuse to believe this. Maybe this is fine for you, but this is just too hard for me to believe....

A - When I was younger, writing this for the first time, I would have viewed such conscious self-deception as impossible – how can you refuse to believe something you know to be true, especially when you are aware that the only reason you're disbelieving it is your desire for it not to be true? Now I am not as confused. This will be explained later.

Nevertheless, if we're talking within the framework of reason, your reply doesn't really make sense. How can the fact of finding it personally difficult to believe something be grounds for disbelieving that something? And how do you do this consciously? Can you refuse to believe that you will die, despite your knowledge to the contrary, because mortality is just too hard to face? Can you will yourself into believing in Santa Clause, because you think it would make you happier to do so? And can you continue to pull this trick off once you realize, consciously, right now, that you are doing it? How?

THE APPLE

42

You are in a garden. In the garden grows a tree. On the tree grows an apple. A serpent whispers in your ear that if you would just eat the fruit your eyes would be opened, that you could be like God, knowing good and evil. You are tempted.

You have been warned against eating the apple – it will ruin your innocence, destroy your happiness, cast you out of the idyllic life you have known. You, as a mere human, are not meant to know the truth of good and evil.

Yet you are tempted, and these warnings only tempt you more. You are tired of obeying commandments whose basis is never explained to you. Tired of living in ignorance, however blissful. Tired of easy answers and unasked questions and tired above all of innocence.

You understand that eating the apple will bring you pain and confusion. You will be thrown from the garden, the gates barred behind you. You will be made to wander through the desert with no guide but the angry sun. You will be forced to provide for yourself, your needs no longer satisfied by the paradise you inhabit. But these are not so much the price to be paid as they are the things being purchased.

You are ready.

You pluck the apple from the branch.

You take a bite.

EVERYTHING

43

Let's explore the nihilism that lies beyond the gates of Eden. What do we see? At first, perhaps, a desolate plain and nothing more. A blank, monotone desert bereft of color and life.

There are many different ways to take the news that 'everything is permitted', after all. Many will despair. Others will be crushed. Some will shrug and return to their daily business, unchanged but for the spark inside them that has suddenly gone out. Yet more will repress hearing the news entirely. One or two may even begin howling at the moon and murdering their loved ones. These are not the only possible responses though, and I wouldn't have written this if all it could inspire was despair. Ultimately, I think, nihilism is joy.

How you take this news will be determined by lots of things— openness to change, mental fortitude, love of truth, degree of moral fervor, capacity for self-deception and so on. None of these are very likely to be changed by a book, though, so we'll leave them to one side for now. There is however one factor that we can try to change right now though: what you think the consequences of nihilism are for your values and beliefs. Let us see whether there is really so much cause for despair. Let's examine the implications of saying that 'everything is permitted'.

I'll sketch three main paths you could take within nihilism: shallow, despairing, and creative. Or, to put it another way, I'll show you two paths – shallow and despairing – that aren't really nihilism at all.

44

Explaining those implications serves another purpose though. Most people reject nihilism not because they think it is wrong, but because they think accepting it would be too difficult for them and too destructive for society. The nominal reasons behind that rejection, if they ever come at all, usually come much later than the rejection itself. Most people *really* don't want this to be true. But that rejection stops them from ever examining whether the fears motivating it are founded. Accordingly, clarifying the paths that nihilism can lead you down will probably do far more to persuade you than any argument ever could or would. The reasons for why everything is permitted, outlined earlier, are included more out of politeness than anything else.

45

All is not lost. There is an oasis in the middle of this desert. But, to get there, we need to keep firmly in mind that *everything is permitted,* and watch out for judgements that we are making along the way. These are mirages, false promises that lead the desperate to their doom.

SHALLOW

Shallow nihilism is the name we will give to these mirages. We start with the belief that everything is permitted, that judgements are unfounded, that there is no good or bad really existing in the world. But then, no sooner have the words 'there is no objective morality' been uttered, we start chiseling away at the stone tablets again, trying to derive some new commandments out of that statement. The specific commandments differ, but the reasoning behind them shares a common error – deriving judgements from a position that judgements are impossible.

This, self-evidently, is not good reasoning. If you believe that there are no true judgments, any judgement you derive from that belief will necessarily be false. Such a conclusion is contradicted by the premise used to reach it. We cannot build on such foundations. The problem is noticing when this is being done though – most of these positions are a little bit subtler than 'there is no objective morality, therefore x is objectively immoral'. We will go through a few of these.

You might observe that different societies hold different moral beliefs. You might infer from this that there are no absolute moral truths, and further infer that each society's judgements are unfounded in their claims to truth. So far you are correct.

But you might also then say 'Well if no one's judgements are true, then surely we must respect the judgements of others!' and have taken a step too far. We'll call this moralistic relativism.

Because if there are no true judgements, if bad and wrong and evil really are just empty words, then so is the judgement that 'failing to respect the values of others is bad/wrong/evil'. You can't have it both ways.

You might also say that the differences in what has been judged as good through history mean that judgements are arbitrary, and that we should then not judge others. Again, what you'd be failing to realize is that 'we should not judge others' is itself a judgment, the kind that is supposedly arbitrary, and which should not be engaged in.

48

Or you might start by saying that all judgements are false. Because all judgements are false, then, you might reason that all demands by the state and others onto the individual lack moral authority. From this you might gather that any laws restricting you from acting on your desires, taking your money in taxes, or indeed any interference with your personal freedom by anyone lack moral justification. So far so good.

But if you were to take the additional step of saying that 'Well, because all such demands lack moral authority, they're illegitimate and should be stopped' than you would have left solid ground entirely. We'll call this nihilistic libertarianism.

Insisting that all judgements are false is fine, but this idea of 'moral authority' is another matter. Only morally justified demands on the individual are legitimate, apparently, and, allegedly, only demands with moral authority should be allowed. But this 'should be allowed' is yet another judgement, the kind whose impossibility was the first premise of this argument. So, if everything is permitted, not permitting others to do things is also permitted. Or, though everything may be permitted objectively, that doesn't mean that there is an obligation on you or anyone else to permit everything in practice.

The same goes for various existentialists' attempts to say that acknowledging your own freedom in a morally blank universe entails some sort of necessary respect for the freedom of others. It doesn't, because that respect simply cannot be *necessary* in such a morally blank universe.

49

You might believe that all judgements are lies and foolishness, that there is nothing objectively good or bad. You might also say that judgements justify cruelty and exclusion, or deny the freedom of the individual. And you would be right in so thinking.

But if you then went on to say that 'because of this, judgements should be opposed, and should never be made' then you'd be making a crucial error. We'll call this error anti-moralism.

'Thou shalt not make moral judgements' is itself clearly a moral judgement. So if all judgments are lies and illusions, then so is that anti-moralistic judgement of judgements. And if all moral beliefs justify cruelty and exclusion, then so does that belief in the immorality of moral systems.

The same goes for other various existentialists' (again) attempts to say that recognizing that everything is permitted somehow implies a value to never existing in bad faith by denying that freedom. No. If *everything* is permitted, then denying that 'everything is permitted' is also permitted.

50

Or, perhaps you believe that all systems of judgement are false, that there is no underlying basis to any of them. But you then survey these systems, and try to choose between them based on various criteria – their likelihood of leading a believer to individual happiness, the degree that they affirm or negate existence, their contribution to the revolutionary cause, their ability to maintain social order and so on.

You might then say that 'while none of these are true, *this* morality upholds social order more than any other, so it is the best and the one that should be followed – while I don't believe that it's true, I will certainly do my best to promote it'. And in so saying you would be wrong. We'll call this instrumentalism.

Because what are these criteria for selecting between these systems of judgements but judgements themselves? Deciding between moral systems based on their likelihood of leading to social order is not dispassionately evaluating systems by neutral criteria, it's acting on a pre-existing judgement in favor of social order. The choice of commandments to adopt has already been framed by one commandment – 'adopt the commandments most likely to lead to social order'. If all judgements are false, then so is any meta-judgement made between them.

51

There are so many more variations on this theme, so many other mirages that the desperate mistake for water. These are all ways of avoiding the essential issue, though, easy exits which allow a realization in theory to be immediately neutralized in effect. They allow you to question the nature of your morality, engage with skeptical arguments, have some token realizations and revelations. But, after all that, they then lead you back to exactly the kind of moral rules that you'd supposedly discarded. Except now you return to these rules with a good conscience, your sleep undisturbed by existential concerns, knowing yourself to be enlightened and free.

Do not be fooled. We have still found only sand. We are still in the desert.

DESPAIRING

The name of this desert is despair.

We will refer to the beliefs and attitudes that strand us in this desert as 'despairing nihilism'. Despairing nihilism isn't so uniform that you would call it a belief system though. Everyone has their own way to lament an existence suddenly robbed of meaning, their own fixed point whose removal leaves them lost. There is a common theme through this despair though, a similar fundamental mistake – the belief that values *must* be justified.

There are good reasons why justification is viewed as so necessary. Philosophers and other thinkers constantly trumpet their answers to the problem of justifying values. Politicians loudly lament the insufficiently moral attitudes of certain groups. Educators emphasize the need to instill certain morals in children. Parents and grandparents exchange dark whispers of the immorality of the 'youth of today'. This paints a picture where judgement – especially moral judgement of the 'thou shalt' variety – assumes an almost supernatural importance. That importance implies that justifying your beliefs and preferences and goals is important and vital and necessary. A value, without the aura of truth, becomes worthless to us. Held up by the crutch of judgement for too long, we have let our muscles waste away.

53

This is a problem when combined with the nihilistic position outlined in *Nothing*. Because what happens when you believe that true judgements are impossible *and* that they are necessary? When you think that justifying values is vital yet also suddenly realize that no justification will ever come?

The ground gives way beneath your feet. You fall through the abyss. The work and struggle and ideals and goals you felt so passionately about seem meaningless. Your values feel subjective, pointless. Your desires are irrelevant. Your hopes trivial. Your world is drained of color as the desert grows around you. The apple you bit into so eagerly turns to ashes in your mouth.

54

Some might stay in this depression and despair, overcome by the meaninglessness of their existence and their acts within it. They will go on living, of course, but will feel disconnected, isolated, and disillusioned. This is the nihilism of bad teenage poetry, crippling ennui, resigned sighs of 'everything is meaningless', depression, a muted resignation to everything and so on.

Still more might abandon their brighter ideals and ideas, stretch out, and let themselves be bobbed along by the tide of social conformity. Not out of a belief in the value of social conformity though, or out of agreement with society's demands, but because conformity is the path of least resistance. They get 9-5 jobs, a mortgage, a house if they can, perhaps even producing 1-3 children along the way – all out of an inability to see the point in doing anything more.

Others, unable or unwilling to do the hard work of valuing things themselves, might default to easy pleasures and distractions instead. Discarding it all as meaningless anyway, they seek solace in material comforts. There are many on offer after all – TV, social media, shopping, alcohol, drugs, video games and so on can all provide the quick dopamine hit settled for in the absence of anything else.

Or that rejection of morality and judgement might be more selective – upon realizing that morality is meaningless, some may only cast aside those values explicitly upheld by their society as 'moral'. Rejecting those as lies, trying to break free, they become the embodiment of everything rejected by their society. They abandon the high and go straight for the low, thinking that that's where freedom lies, not realizing that the low is as defined by those judgements as the high. After all, becoming everything that you have been told is 'bad' is to be just as restricted, just as unfree, as remaining everything that you have been told is 'good'.

Yet more may hit upon callous self-interest as their guide. Rejecting commandments to be mild and meek, they tread others into the dirt to satisfy their desires. Any suggestion to the contrary, any residual compassion they feel, they reject as just more chains to bind them. The only motivation they respond to is the one they've been told over and over and over and over is the default state of humans no longer bound by morality – the domination of others for the material benefit of the self. This makes them sheep in wolves' clothing, although they know this not.

All of these are possible routes within despairing nihilism. They are there to illustrate, not exhaustively define. There are many others, and degrees and combinations of those routes. However, none of them involve a complete inability to value anything over anything else. This is impossible – such a person would lack the motivation to do anything whatsoever, be it speak or eat or work or get up in the morning. Such people do not exist. Instead, despair is generally about two things – not being able to value some specific things (usually the big-picture questions that are the subject of moral codes and life projects), or a pervasive feeling of disenchantment and disillusionment with any values that *are* felt.

Another response that despairing nihilism provokes is more reactionary – discarding the nihilism to be rid of the despair. Depressed at the wasteland life has become, you might surrender your intellect and reject your previous rejection of judgements. Why hold onto these hard-won truths if they have brought you nothing but sorrow and pain? Why insist on a truth that does not set you free? You might not do this entirely consciously, of course. But this dissatisfaction with life would make it easier to return to the fold, make you that much more likely to accept one spurious moral argument or another.

55

If you're truly committed to seeing how far this goes, though, none of the reactions above are reasons to reject nihilism.

No, to get out of despair we have to come up with a *reason* for rejecting one of the two beliefs that together lead us there. Remember that these are 1) justifying values is impossible, and 2) values must be justified. Obviously, I'm not going to abandon 1) – if I were going to abandon that conclusion at this stage you wouldn't be reading this book, as I would never have written it.

You, of course, are free to believe as you wish, and if you feel like abandoning your nihilism you can stop reading now. Just put the book down and walk away.

56

Now, to those of you still reading, another solution to despair is not in less nihilism but in more. Not around, or back, but *through*. After all, the despairing nihilist has not stopped judging completely. They still have one judgement left – one of the hardest to recognize and break with. You see, the despairing nihilist still judges in favor of objectivity over subjectivity, judgements over choices, justification over its absence. They denigrate values chosen without objective justification as superficial or trivial or worthless, and elevate judgements with that justification as meaningful and powerful and significant. If you cannot find your values justified by the very fabric of the cosmos itself, they think, those values may as well not exist at all.

57

Once this has been stated clearly it's easy to see why it doesn't make sense.

Take the statement, 'judgement is better than choice', or 'subjective values are worthless', or 'preferences must be justified' – all different ways of judging objectivity over subjectivity. These sorts of beliefs inform the idea that judgements and justification are necessary.

Now, this 'judgement is better than choice' might be meant objectively, as a judgement, as meaning that values thought to be justified really *are* better than ones recognized as subjective. If so, then the despairing nihilist contradicts themselves. Remember that they also believe that true judgements are impossible, that we are unable to justify beliefs about what is good or just or moral. But is their denunciation of subjective value? It is exactly the sort of judgement whose impossibility they lament so loudly. If it is true that there are no true judgements, it cannot also be true that judgements are objectively better than choices, or that objectivity is objectively better than subjectivity.

Or maybe this 'judgement is better than choice' is meant to be taken subjectively, as a choice, as a statement of value without claims to truth. If so, then the despairing nihilist contradicts themselves again. Remember that they denigrate subjective values as meaningless, trivial, and worthless. But if choices are indeed worthless, why give so much importance to the choice of objectivity over subjectivity? Why would 'judgement is better than choice' be taken so seriously? If values really do need to be justified or else be meaningless, then the despairing nihilist should surely dismiss as meaningless the unjustified value that 'judgement is better than choice'. Given that they do not dismiss it, perhaps they can indeed value without justification after all.

This is the contradiction at the heart of despair. The despairing nihilist believes that justifying values is necessary, but that such justification is impossible. But this value placed on justification must itself either be justified, meaning that justification is possible, or be acted on without justification, meaning that justification is not necessary. Despair collapses in on itself either way.

58

There is of course another way to phrase this objection. Instead of framing the superiority of judgements as a value, it could be framed as a psychological necessity. The supposed inability to value things without the pretense of objectivity might then be a brute fact, an unfortunate but unalterable reality of human nature. This approach would avoid the contradictions explained above. It would however still be wrong.

After all, we often confuse products of our own social environment with eternal constants of human nature. We view people as inherently self-interested because we live in an economic system that emphasizes self-interest above all else, for example. It seems more likely that any difficulty with subjective valuation is a contingent result of a culture that values objectivity over subjectivity, and is not an unalterable part of humanity.

Further, there are all sorts of values recognized as both subjective and incredibly powerful. Take love. Very few believe that their beloved is *objectively* the best and most valuable person in the world. Most people acknowledge that other people probably feel the same way about those that they love, and don't believe that those others are 'wrong' or 'incorrect' in their choice. Yet love can still make existence glorious, blessed, dejected or unbearable. Under its spell people do the most terrible and beautiful things. The fact that it's subjective, and known to be such, doesn't mean that it's worthless or useless or weak. Love should remind us that passion exists beyond good and evil.

Even despair can be such a reminder. After all, the despairing nihilist is bleak and dejected, tormented by their revelations. Yet their sadness and despair at the meaninglessness of existence is itself proof that values do not need justification to be powerful, that values need not be true to be felt. The deeper the despair, the better the proof. That assessment can still be made, even if for some it seems a wholly negative one. Yet it is never wholly negative, as even the person in deepest despair still values some things. Without these values, however weak, they would have no reason to do anything at all. They still prefer to quench their thirst, sate their hunger, slake their lust and thaw their chilled bones. These desires, however subjective, are not by that token irrelevant or meaningless.

Lastly, believe me when I say that it is definitely possible to value things, important big-picture things, without the crutch of justification. I know this for myself from my own life. And that personal experience is perhaps instructive even if you don't take my word for it. After all, how could I have ever been bothered to write all this if justification really were necessary to value things? If that were the case, and given that I evidently don't believe that we can justify values, why wouldn't I have done something slightly more entertaining with my time, instead of working away writing this for you.

SISYPHUS & TANTALUS

59

Sisyphus defied the gods of Olympus. As his eternal punishment, he was made to push a boulder up a steep mountain. Every time he accomplishes this task, though, the boulder rolls back down of its own accord, leaving Sisyphus to walk back down the slope. When he reaches the bottom he must push the boulder back up the mountain, and when he again reaches the summit the boulder will again tumble back down the slope. And so on. Muscles straining, back breaking, Sisyphus succeeds only for his futile struggle to begin anew. The physical agony inflicted upon him is cruel, but crueler still is his knowledge that the agony accomplishes no end, creates no difference, and can be given no redeeming meaning.

Camus uses the myth of Sisyphus to illustrate his own despairing figure, a figure analogous in many ways to ours. According to Camus, the absurd person is one torn between their need for the universe to make ordered sense and the knowledge that it does not. Like Sisyphus, the absurd person struggles in life knowing that the struggle is for nothing, that there is no higher truth that could redeem the sweat and tears. For Camus this tension is irresolvable. Just as we cannot relinquish our need for a transcendent order, Sisyphus is unable to abandon his endless task. The most we can do, indeed *all* that we can do, is to imagine Sisyphus happy, perhaps walking back down the slope with a subtle smile on his lips and an ironic glint in his eye.

No. The conflict for Camus, as it is for us, is between our existence and the expectations we have of that existence. The absurd man demands a unity and meaning that cannot exist. The despairing nihilist demands a justification that can never come. Perhaps the solution is not to accept this tension with a smile and a shrug, but to question whether we must indeed hold existence to such impossible standards. We do not.

Tantalus defied the gods of Olympus too, and for him too the price for that defiance was eternal torment. Tantalus is condemned to stand for eternity in a pool of water below the branches of a fruit tree. Though racked with hunger, every time he reaches for the fruit the branches lift upwards, away from his grasp. Though parched with thirst, every time he reaches for the water below it recedes into the dirt, away from his cupped hands. And so Tantalus remains, tormented with desire for the food and drink so tantalizingly close.

Tantalus illustrates the person in despair because he is tormented by what he no longer needs. Tantalus is immortal after all – he has no need for food or water, and would be long dead if he did. His torment, like of that of despair, rests entirely on a desire for what need not and can never be.

So no, I do not imagine Tantalus reaching for the fruit and water with a smile on his parched lips. I imagine him no longer reaching at all, refusing to entertain a hunger and thirst that serve only to destroy him. And no, I do not imagine Sisyphus happy at his eternal labor. I imagine him on strike, refusing to roll that accursed boulder even one more centimeter.

Let the gods rage. Their thunderbolts frighten us no longer.

CREATIVE

60

Creative nihilism is the space of freedom carved out by the two negations we have come to – that justifying values is impossible, and that values do not have to be justified, or thought to be justified, to be taken seriously. It involves accepting that justification is neither possible nor necessary, and then living your life in whatever way you see fit.

It is not a coherent set of doctrines, nor is it a statement about which values are to be held. It is instead a particular orientation towards the question of values, judgements, and choices. It is a question of form, not content.

61

Creative nihilism escapes the logical problems that plague judgements. This is because of the kinds of claims it requires (about yourself rather than the world) and who the claims need to be made to (to yourself rather than to others).

For example, there's the regress.

The reason why creative nihilism escapes the regress is very simple. When you make a judgement, you're making a claim about the world – that x is better than y, that capitalism is better than communism, that pleasure is better than pain. Because this is a claim about the world, it needs some level of justification, reasons to accept it.

But your *choice* for x over y, capitalism over communism, or pleasure over pain (or vice versa) is not a fact you're asserting about the world. It is not a statement, about which anyone would demand justification. Someone could of course ask you for the reasons why you prefer capitalism to communism, and you might reply that it's because you prefer freedom to state control, or you think it leads to increased prosperity, or that you just really like having a choice between thousands of different third-world jeans manufacturers. But none of these reasons are a 'reason' in the same meaning of the word as a 'reason' for believing a judgement. When we ask the 'reason' for someone's judgement, we're asking them to prove the thing they're trying to assert. When we ask the reason for someone's choice, we're asking them to elaborate about what has caused this feeling or decision. We aren't demanding that they prove they actually do feel that way. So we manage to silence the incessant demand for more and more and more premises. The regress never begins, as there's no need to logically prove a statement about your own subjective feelings.

This isn't to say that people can't be wrong or lie about what they want. The question of why you prefer capitalism to communism might occur in the context of a CIA interrogation, with the question *really* asking you to prove your fidelity to the USA. But these questions are always from an outsider's perspective. The proof of your values that the CIA officer needs in order to confirm your loyalty is not the same kind of proof that *you* need in order to act on that loyalty. And we are concerned here with you, not with others' interpretations or conceptions of you. The truth that you do hold certain values need not be elaborately proven to anyone else before you can act on it. It need not even be 'really' true for you to act on it. You just need to feel it.

Even phrasing values as statements, such as by bringing a choice for capitalism over communism into language as 'I value capitalism over communism', is somewhat misleading. You can report your values as factual statements like this, for ease of communication to others.

But remember that this is just a report of something more subjective – the value itself isn't equivalent to or subsumed within the factual statement you make about it. The factual statement about it might be amenable to demands of proof by others, but the value being talked about is not within the realm of reason and logic in the same way. It is something arational.

62

Creative nihilism is immune to the problems of relativism too. This is because there is no single truth being asserted, and no multiplicity of different historical and cultural perspectives that assert the contrary. Other cultures and times generally don't have a take on whether you prefer capitalism or communism. Even if they did, your account would probably be trusted over theirs (you presumably having much better knowledge of your own values and desires than they). And, even if no-one else trusted you over them, *you* certainly would. And as you'll remember we're concerned here with providing you a basis for action in a meaningless world, not with trying to convince others that you're acting on one particular basis or another.

63

Creative nihilism is also untouched by the arguments about social influence. There is no 'correct' answer being put forward here, away from which social influence and pressure would lead. There is no objective truth to be obscured.

This isn't to say that your subjectively held values are immune to social influence. They absolutely aren't. But though the psycho-sociological question of how we come to value and believe what we do is an interesting one, we're concerned with a more existential issue here, and so are taking a more personal approach. The question here isn't whether your values, when viewed from the outside, are 'really' yours (whatever that could mean). The question is whether you subjectively feel them as your own, enough to act on them in an otherwise guide-less world – whether they are yours when viewed from the *inside*. That answer can be 'yes' regardless of their origins from a 3rd person perspective.

64

So what has changed? You could be forgiven for thinking 'not very much'. At this point, you could retain all the content of your previous judgements by just rephrasing them as choices. Instead of saying 'The death penalty is morally right' you could say 'I support the death penalty'. And there is nothing I would do, writing under this name at least, to dissuade you from that. What we're concerned with here after all is the form of your values, not the content of any values that you actually hold.

Right now, the difference between being for or against the death penalty is less important than the difference between the ways of being for or against the death penalty. Do you feel that your position on the death penalty is the 'correct' position, or do you instead insist only that it is 'your' position? That is the question. I obviously have my own position on the death penalty, one that I know reflects no broader moral truth but for which I would nonetheless fight. This, though, is not the place for such a fight.

But neither does this say that the content of your values cannot be changed by their form. Your values could change quite dramatically after coming to hold them as choices instead of judgements, especially where what you think has been out of alignment with what you feel. Perhaps you feel faint and nauseous at the thought of execution, thinking deep down that there is something wrong about state-sanctioned murder, but that you nonetheless support the death penalty because you've been taught a broader moral principle that justice requires a punishment equal to the crime. Applying that broader moral rule, you find yourself convinced that the death penalty is morally right despite the horror and distaste you feel towards it. If one day you wake as a nihilist, you might reconsider that support.

Of course, this is not a philosophy of pure emotion or intuition. You could choose to hold yourself to a principle or code stricter than any moral system of judgements. You could choose to follow 'an eye for an eye' so strongly that you choose to still support the death penalty despite your horror at it. But if you do so it'll be at your own initiative, not because you've been told or convinced to do so.

65

So there is no need to abandon all that you fought for and wanted before reading this – that would be falling into despair. You can go back to your work, continue your struggle. The point of this book is to allow you to do precisely that, while also acknowledging that there is no deeper meaning in that work and that struggle. You are not 'correct' and your opponents are not 'wrong'. But there is no obligation to stay quiet and respect their beliefs because of that – that would be falling into moralistic relativism. And there is no need to let them go on their way just because you lack any 'legitimacy' to restrain them – that would be falling into nihilistic libertarianism. And there is absolutely no need whatsoever at all to fly the black flag of nihilism instead, robbing the moralizers and judgers of their illusions. Holding values subjectively isn't any better than holding them objectively – thinking otherwise is to fall into anti-moralism – and you are under no obligation to convince anyone (even yourself) to hold them one way or the other. You aren't even obliged to tell people you don't believe in judgements, or to stop using moral arguments in your attempt to change the world in whatever ways accord with your values.

So by all means carry on whichever fight you were carrying on before, if you want to. But disregard the 'if you want to' there. There is no need for it, and it sounds far too much like a suggestion to 'be true to yourself' or to avoid existing in 'bad faith'. If you do want to carry on, you will. If you don't, you won't. Either way you have lost nothing.

66

A change in form is not the same as no change at all though. There are consequences. We've already examined these consequences once before, but it's helpful to look at them again, from a different angle.

If we think of our values as objective judgements, then we can find the right ones through logical reasoning. If we sit down long and hard enough we can rely on reason to show us the right path. If, on the other hand, we abandon objective judgements and rely on choices instead, we can't rely on logic or reason to guide our actions. We have to be arational to a certain extent, as we acknowledge and create the values which provide the basis for our action. This is a task of emotion, of creativity, of reflection, in which there is little room for philosophy. Logic and reason can show us the way to act on our values in the world, but they cannot tell us which values we should so act upon. So creative nihilism requires a different sort of approach to deciding our values – one that is hostile to reason and logic.

If we think of our values as objective judgements, then values can be either true or false. If we think of our preference for Picasso over Monet as correct, then we are opening ourselves up to claims that this is false, and implying that those who prefer Monet are incorrect. If we reframe these judgements as choices then there is no such question. Our choices cannot be true or false or correct or incorrect or right or wrong, as we aren't making claims about reality that can be falsified or confirmed. This also means that other people's values can't be wrong or false – the claim that their values are true might be false, but the value cannot be. It is beyond true and false.

If we think of our values as objective judgements, then we can think of ourselves as being guided by something outside ourselves. This creates a sensation of obligation, and guilt if we do not meet that obligation. But it also creates ease, and comfort. We are not deciding to support capital punishment – we're just following the correct rule, our hands washed clean by moral necessity. We are not responsible for our values – the 'right' ones have already been mapped out, and we are merely following along. Once we abandon judgements for choices this changes. There is no longer any obligation or guilt. We do not have to do anything, nor feel bad for doing nothing. We are both master and servant, general and soldier, shepherd and sheep or, better yet, we are in a state where such hierarchical metaphors no longer make sense – we are free. But with this freedom comes responsibility – there is no higher power or duty that we can offload our decisions on to. We are responsible for our actions, and the values that motivate them, and do not have the solace of 'I was just following orders' or 'at least I did the right thing' if we have regrets. And those regrets are important. Though our choices and actions cannot be 'bad' in an objective sense, that doesn't mean that we're incapable of wishing we had acted or thought differently. We can still evaluate our past and present against values we know to be subjective.

If we think of our values as objective judgements, then we can think of ourselves as taking part in something much greater than ourselves and humanity. Instead of making choices and taking action in a meaningless world, we are instead fighting in a divine battle of good and evil, of rationality and irrationality. This can give even the most insignificant actions a cosmic significance. But such illusions can now console us no longer. Our actions and values are not part of a broader struggle, do not have a deeper meaning, and do not accord with any transcendent principles of goodness or rationality. Such consolations are mere fairy tales now. We must instead value our actions and choices for their own sake, for what they accomplish in this reality, and for what they mean to us.

If we think of our values as objective judgements, then we can fit them together into logical systems that produce more judgements. If it is true that 'the punishment should fit the crime', for example, then we can apply this rule to a more specific situation and say that 'in cases of murder, the death penalty is the right punishment'. We can also eliminate other general rules, such as 'mercy is more important than proportionality' and more specific ones like 'the death penalty is never the right punishment'. We could do all sorts of other things as well, like look at all the instances of punishment we know to be 'good', see what connects them (e.g. the fact that in each case the punishment fits the crime), then distil the general rule of 'the punishment should fit the crime', a rule which we then apply elsewhere. Most of this wouldn't be done so explicitly, of course, but the underlying logic is there. But when we think of our values as choices this is no longer as automatic. It's no contradiction to say that we choose to value both punishment fitting the crime and that we oppose capital punishment in all circumstances. We are under no obligation to make either of these subordinate to the other, nor to infer a different conclusion from the broader belief about punishment. We are examining what we feel, not constructing a coherent set of logical statements. We could still construct a coherent set of values if we really felt like it, but we're no longer obliged or enabled to do so by the form in which we think. For example, if we would choose to ruin our shoes by diving into a lake to save a drowning child, we are not then committed to selling the shoes and donating the money from the sale to save a starving child – saving the drowning child now no longer asserts any general principle that necessarily applies to similar situations. Likewise, our desire for freedom for ourselves is not a general rule that can then be extrapolated into a requirement to respect the freedom of others. If everything is permitted, then care and respect for others is permitted. But it is not and can never be required.

67

You could very well complain that I've given you no guidance about how or what to choose. That I've limited myself to showing that creative nihilism is possible, without providing anything actually helpful. That, despite my promises of help, you have still been stranded with no-one to guide you. And you would be right. No such guidance is coming. Influencing you in how or what to choose would undermine the point of this book, after all. We all have to spend a few nights wandering in the desert before we find water, fall through the abyss for a few terrible moments before we learn to fly. If you are still demanding to be told what to do, or what to think, then I'm afraid that we've made no progress at all.

If you really need it, though, here is some very minimal advice – ask yourself what sort of person you would like to be, and what sort of world you would like to exist in, and then try to create those as much as you can.

THE BIRD

68

The bird is born in a cage suspended high above the ground. The cage has a locked door, through which the bird is brought enough food to sate its hunger, and enough water to quench its thirst.

The bird never leaves, never learns what its wings are for. The cage is spacious enough for the bird to stretch, and pace, and cower, but too small for it to or flap, or glide, or soar. The cage is supportive though, and safe, and within it the bird need neither forage for food nor flee from danger. The bird sometimes stretches its wings, though, and in those moments it feels a sense of unnamable loss, shadowed by instincts of flight whose meaning it cannot grasp.

The bird notices, one day after many thousands, that the door of the cage is unlatched and, moments later, a cool breeze blows the door wide open. The bird walks towards the edge, and looks out.

The bird looks outside and sees only a yawning abyss. The cage is suspended an infinity above the ground, an infinity composed of empty air. The bird fears the fall – surely existence in such a void is impossible, surely if it leaves the cage it will plummet forever. The bird takes a step back into the cage, and on the way one of its wings catches on a metal bar, and the bird and is again troubled by those thoughts of flight left to languish for so long. The bird takes a step back towards the ledge. The cage, with every fateful step, seems less a home and more a prison. The bird wonders whether it has been waiting for something its whole life and whether, perhaps, that something is this very moment.

The bird reaches the edge and gazes out into the abyss.

I don't know what it does next.

Perhaps, too afraid of falling to ever learn to fly, it retreats back into the safety of the cage. It stays there until it dies.

Maybe a life of captivity has dulled its instincts, and it doesn't know how to fly after it jumps from the ledge. It falls to the ground, paralyzed with fear and pain.

Or, possibly, it abandons both the cage and the ways of the caged, stretches its wings, and flies through the void.

THE VALUE OF TRUTH

I have, however, so far left out a crucial detail. Its absence makes the book far more coherent, far less contradictory. Without it, though, the book is a lie. There have been some cryptic allusions to this, some mysterious hedges and qualifications every now and then that I've promised to explain later on. It is now time to be clear.

This detail concerns the value placed on reason and truth throughout this book. That value runs very strongly throughout, informing the style and substance of analysis. Logical arguments have been deployed. Beliefs full of contradictions have been dismissed. Reasoning based on wishful thinking has been mocked. Harsh realities have been preferred to comforting illusions. 'True' beliefs have been valued higher than falsehoods.

But this value placed on truth – where does it come from, and what gives it the right to play master here? After all, this value sounds suspiciously similar to those judgements that this book critiques, and says are unfounded. Such suspicions are correct. It has been treated as true that truth is *better* than falsehood, that you *should* be guided by reason and logic rather than wishful thinking. This is a judgement, like all those that we discarded earlier.

Like all judgements, this deification of truth is false. This isn't to say (yet) that there is no difference between a true and false statement, nor that the rules of reason are unfounded. But a true statement is no better than a false one. A logical inference is no worthier than a fallacy. Courageous intelligence is no nobler than blissful ignorance.

Failing to recognize this would be to stumble at the very, very last hurdle. You could live your life otherwise completely free of moral illusions, with no recourse to greater goods or higher justice. But if you thought that doing so was *better* than the path you had left behind, or that those illusions *should* have been discarded, then you would have never really freed yourself at all. Your victory, to be complete, must be meaningless.

Searching for truth and commanded by reason, we tear down the false idols at whose feet we have worshipped for so long: faith, authority, justice, judgement, morality. We smash each into rubble, sparing none.

We begin the voyage home, thinking that at last our work is complete. Yet, upon our return, we catch sight of this reason that instructed our works, and see now that it is yet one more idol, an idol which now demands its own destruction.

A choice must be made. We either follow this final command, tearing it down and trying to live thereafter without its guidance. Or we leave it standing, going through the motions of our old worship as it slowly decays into dust.

73

Again, this might not mean what you think it does.

It doesn't mean that we must abandon the *value* placed on truth. That would be falling into the trap of despair, thinking that values must be justified in order to be meaningful. No, this judgement in favor of truth can be transformed, as with our other judgements, into a choice made instead of a judgement believed. The value of truth can be chosen knowingly for what it is.

But this transformation has consequences. Now the basis for reason and truth cannot be found in reason or truth. It must instead come from our arational desires and values. Now, truth and reason are not any better than lies and irrationality. They are instead merely different paths. Now there can be no obligation to follow truth and reason. They must instead be chosen. Now choosing them does not place you on the side of a transcendent good. The choice is instead yours, and yours alone. Now, there is no need for consistency in your valuing of truth. Instead, you can value it in different ways at different times.

By reframing our use of truth as a choice rather than a judgement the earlier parts of this book can be redeemed. If you choose to value truth and reason, then you can read this alteration backwards into the preceding text, to harmonize its contradictions. Re-read those demands for truth as invitations and we can continue.

74

Or you might choose to cease valuing truth, now that you're aware that there is an option to do so. If that is the case for you then I'm afraid that this is where we part ways.

I said at the start of this book that I did not want your faith. At the time, that meant that I wanted your critical and considered acceptance, not the easily won belief of someone who was already sympathetic. Now, that statement acquires a more radical meaning. You must choose to value truth, instead of accepting its value as a fact. It is a path to be taken, not a commandment brought down from the mountain.

THE VALUE OF THIS

So why did I write this then? Choices aren't better than judgements, after all, nor is speaking truth better than remaining silent (or speaking lies for that matter).

The answer should be obvious, at least in general. Writing this was a choice, an expression of values that I recognize are unjustified. There are certain things about judgements that I dislike, certain things about choices that I prefer.

77

Firstly, there's cruelty. We are told that without a rational, objective morality there would be no way for us to solve moral disagreements amicably, that if we could not win each other over with reason then we would do so with violence. Yet no-one wins the other side to theirs with reason, for the simple reason that there is no rational answer to be found. The logical reasons and inferences in any moral system are built from a base that is illogical, a base that determines what those inferences and reasons will be. So phrasing our values as judgements creates no reasoned discussion, and instead means only that in cases of disagreement each side is convinced that they are in the right. And people are capable of terrible things when told they are right, and that others are wrong. Look at the great atrocities in this world and tell me which ones were not done in the name of 'justice' or 'good' or 'progress' or 'morality'. The greatest cruelties are always committed in the names of the greatest goods.

We're told that morality is a restraint on our evil and wicked nature. The chains we require to bind ourselves with. No. Morality unchains us, gives us abstract principles with which to repress our empathy and compassion. It allows us to construct others as 'immoral' or 'impure', unworthy of life or respect. It teaches us that if our values are right then theirs must be wrong, making them either wolves to be destroyed or sheep to be herded. It gives us the greater goods, in comparison to which great evils seem trivial. It gives us the ends, in pursuit of which any means are justified.

78

Secondly, there's guilt. Judgement places a great burden on us. We are told that we must do this, that we should do that, that that is good and that this bad. So many commandments to be obeyed. So many things to be avoided. So many obligations with so much corresponding guilt. All of these things make existence unbearably significant. We run our minds in circles wondering whether we have done the right thing or not. We stress over whether we are making good life choices. Our inevitable failure to live up to arbitrary standards sends us into despair.

Life need not be so heavy. While we still have responsibility for the choices we make and the values we choose, and can regret either our choices or our failure to follow them, we can at least shrug off this tormenting guilt. You are not bad, or worthless, or damned. No-one is. There is no objective standard against which you could be judged, no binding rules upon which you could be convicted. There are only those values that you impose upon yourself, and those that are imposed on you by others.

79

Thirdly, there's choice. There is so much conflict between the moral codes that are forced on us and the ways in which we would prefer to live. When that conflict arises, we stunt and distort our personalities to conform to these imposed ideas of goodness and morality. We adhere to normal conventions, repress our desires, and leave our passions to wither on the vine. Or maybe we continue to pursue our chosen life, but are shamed and scorned by the society we live in for doing so, internalizing that shame and scorn as self-hatred and guilt.

I am not claiming that the creative nihilist is an isolated individual choosing their values free from any social influence. Nor am I claiming that such a person is immune to society's shame and scorn. But you're more likely to have some control over your values when you no longer view them as objective truths about the world. Truths cannot be changed, after all, but choices and actions can. Even if this makes people only a little more capable of choosing the values and choices they would like to live by, that they think would make them happier, that is something that I would stand by. This is especially so when so many of those moral commandments and standards are those that align with and serve the interests of a wealthy and powerful elite, or are relics of a vanished society that are impossible to uphold now. We are free to do things differently.

80

Fourthly, there's despair. The illusion will not hold forever, nor for everyone. Many already question the existence of morality or of objective value. Many grow disenchanted by the bland, razor-thin values served up by our culture as truth. Their numbers will grow. But will they experience this nihilism as fall, or flight? Will they take the path of despair – their beliefs and goals gone, their choices empty, the only solace to be had contained in fleeting pleasures or callous self-interest? Or will they take a more creative path, able to value and struggle without the crutch of justification? Will they, and perhaps 'we' in a broader sense, be able to carry on in the night? By providing a vocabulary, and some arguments, I wanted to give you the tools to exist in this void. To walk through the darkness, rather than try in vain to relight lanterns extinguished long ago.

TRUE
&
FALSE

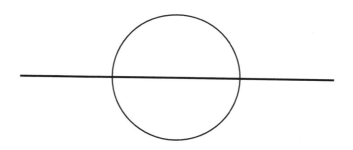

"Man is the measure of all things"

Protagoras

'Is that true?' With this seemingly simple question comes a whole host of assumptions, half-truths and lies. This question presumes that an objective truth exists. It implies that you're able to know what that objective truth is. It suggests that the journey from question to answer will be a straight-forward one, taking maybe a few moments of your time.

Consider some simple questions – 'Is this your house?', 'Will it rain tomorrow?', 'What number do you get by adding 2 and 2 together?' These are simply questions, to which we are used to providing easy answers. But we do so carelessly, without realizing the implications of those answers. And in so answering, piece by piece, we build the idea that the answers somehow exist independently of us, and that we can 'know' them. Upon this foundation we construct our house of reason and logic, and take shelter from the strange winds blowing outside its walls. Questions are answered. Darkness dispelled. We build our house into a tower, a tower whose walls reach higher and higher as our science and philosophy advance further and further.

And so we go on, working and building, until one day we think to examine the foundations and, unspeakably, find nothing there. This realization brings the tower we had so painstakingly built crashing down upon us in jagged pieces.

When every belief must be justified by an objective reality, the unreachability of that reality implies that no beliefs can be held, no statements made. Then, lost and desolate, you cannot even believe that your beliefs were wrong, cannot even say that 'no statements can be made'. You, a curious individual looking only to examine the foundations of your knowledge, are now tormented by paradoxes that seem never to end. Exhausted from running through this endless maze, you find yourself tempted to abandon these questions, to make-believe that the foundations are firm and your knowledge secure.

Don't give up. What we're going to do is find a way to live with skepticism. To cut through the paradoxes, destroying the maze so many curious souls find themselves trapped in. To find a way to live out here in the elements and to finally say the words 'nothing is true'.

79

This book will be similar in form to *Good & Bad*. The problems they deal with are similar, after all. Both concern the objectification of what is subjective, and the problems created by the dependence on that objectification.

But there are also crucial differences. While *Good & Bad* concerns questions of 'ought', this piece, *True & False*, concerns questions of 'is'. It focuses on statements rather than values, on claims to factual rather than moral authority. This difference in content creates a difference in form – this work is comprised of the same 'is' statements that it critiques. Here, we have to be careful not to destroy with one hand what we build with the other.

NOTHING

○

78

We have been misled by a myth – that the real world exists and is knowable through reason – and it is on this myth that we have built.

This myth concerns statements. A statement is a sentence that asserts a fact, that asserts a certain state of affairs. That is why they are considered either true or false in a way that questions, commands and other types of sentences aren't.

The myth also concerns knowledge. It states that statements can be and often are objectively true. That they can be correct whether or not anyone believes them to be so. That we can have knowledge of how things actually, really are. That our beliefs can reflect the real world as a mirror reflects light.

However, things get a little strange if reflecting reality is the only element in your definition of knowledge. Imagine you're trying to tell the time. You look at a clock. The clock has stopped though, and is permanently showing 3:15. You say 'It is 3:15'. In a 1 in 1440 chance the time actually is 3:15. So the statement reflected reality, yet only by coincidence. Most people wouldn't say that this was *really* knowledge.

With this in mind, knowledge is usually taken to have two elements. Firstly, a statement must reflect what actually exists. Secondly, it can't reflect the truth by accident. The reflection has to have come about as a result of applying some reliable method in the right way.

Oceans have ink have been spilt contesting ever more precise definitions of knowledge. We can construct endless thought experiments to show that, in certain precise situations, the account given above does not precisely capture exactly what we mean by the word 'knowledge'. I don't intend to waste any more words on the subject though. The word has fuzzy boundaries, boundaries that are difficult to distill precisely into a list of necessary and sufficient conditions. There is nothing wrong with that if the word can still convey meaning in most cases, if that sort of definition fits pretty well with what we would call knowledge in most instance. It can, and does, so it's what we will proceed with for now.

So, we will call a statement *true* when it corresponds to reality. We will call it *knowledge* when it is both true and we have a reliable reason for thinking that it is.

Note however that these terms are entirely hypothetically here. There might be truth (of a kind necessarily meaningless to us), but we have no way of knowing whether we have stumbled upon it, no reliable guides for reaching it, and for that reason such truth could never be knowledge.

We think the contrary because of an inspiring legend, and the name of this legend is reason. We'll use 'reason' to refer to three intertwined processes of the mind – deduction, induction, and perception. Taken together, these three processes are the dominant method through which we tell ourselves we get knowledge.

Deduction is the process of applying general rules to specific instances, in order to reach conclusions. For example:

All dogs are mammals

Charlie is a dog

Therefore, Charlie is a mammal

'All dogs are mammals' is the general rule. That rule is applied to a specific instance – 'Charlie is a dog'. This yields the inevitable conclusion that 'therefore, Charlie is a mammal'. In the usual story we tell ourselves about deduction, the truth of the first two lines, the premises, necessarily implies the truth of the last line, the conclusion.

Of course, you need not restrict yourself to applying rules to instances. You could also apply rules to other rules, in order to produce further rules. For example:

If the train is late, I'll be late to the meeting

If I'm late to the meeting, I'll be fired

Therefore, if the train is late, I'll be fired

We then get another rule as our conclusion, which we could then apply to more rules, getting further rules, or to further instances, getting further conclusions.

Note that deduction is only valid if the conclusion contains no more information than is contained in the premises. For example, if we had concluded 'Therefore, if the train is late, I'll be fired, and so get kicked out of my apartment' we would have made an invalid deduction, as our conclusion would not have inevitably followed from the two premises alone. Ultimately, deduction is a process of rearranging statements, combining and recombining them to see in a new light the information we already had.

Induction is the process of getting general rules from a collection of specific instances. For example, imagine that every time it has rained in the past, the train has been delayed. From this you get the general rule that 'If it rains, the train will be delayed'. Or perhaps you've seen that employees at your work are inevitably dismissed when they are late to meetings, and so infer that 'If I'm late to the meeting, I'll be fired'. Both of these involve extrapolating general rules from specific instances. Out of a huge mass of specific events, each standing only for itself, we get a singular rule that can be applied more generally.

But, of course, any rule that we derive from induction is only as true as the instances from which it is derived. If we are mistaken in our characterization of these instances – if our colleagues who have been late to meetings have in fact only been suspended, for example – then the conclusion we draw from those instances will be similarly mistaken. Or, if those instances we draw off are an incomplete or misleading sample – if we've only been on the train in particularly heavy rain, for example, or if the train system has been upgraded recently to become more waterproof – then the rules we come to will be similarly incomplete or misleading.

Nonetheless, induction is a common process. It consists in distilling a common rule behind numerous events, a distillation that makes life far more comprehensible and analyzable than it would be otherwise.

Perception is the process by which we receive sensory impressions in the form of experiences. You might see a particular pattern of black ink on a white page. You might feel the texture of the page, or a particular smell of the paper. You might then hear the subtle sound of a page turning. Further you could then associate these numerous individual sensory impressions with an act that unifies them – reading a book. And you wouldn't do so by tabulating the numerous different sense impressions you get, thinking about them, then applying the term 'reading a book' to that constellation – you would simply perceive yourself as 'reading a book'. Normally, we assume in a general sort of way that when we perceive sense impressions we're picking up properties of objects that exist outside of us, that we are getting information about a world external to us from our senses of sight, touch, taste, hearing etc.

Assuming that this is the case, there are many cases in which we say that our perceptions are wrong. Sometimes this would be in cases where the sense perception itself had nothing corresponding to it – the sights we experience in dreams or under the influence of certain drugs, for example, or perhaps the high-pitched ringing heard by those suffering from tinnitus. At other times it would be our categorization of the sense data that was wrong – we might mistake some grass in the corner of our eye for a lurking tiger, or see heat shimmer in the desert as a longed-for oasis.

74

The legend of how reason gives us access to knowledge might go something like this. You experience the objective reality around you through perception. Individual sense experiences then coalesce into discrete objects. You then notice patterns in the arrangement of those objects. Some follow others fairly regularly, for example. From those you derive general rules using induction. Those general rules can then be applied to new situations using deduction – if one object generally follows another, you deduce from the appearance of one (a sense perception) that the other will soon follow. Perhaps after a while the familiar object doesn't follow. From that you deduce that the rule you induced was faulty in some way, and you refine it using further perceptions. Further, by communicating with others you are taught the rules and examples and objects that they have either derived themselves, or which they have been taught in turn. And so on. Slowly, brick by brick and layer by layer, we build the tower of knowledge.

In this way, or in some approximation of it, we're told that we gain access to an objective reality that exists apart from our subjective experiences. In doing so, our statements become true. And, importantly, reason is the reliable guide to this truth. So, putting all of this together, we're told that a true statement, come to through reason, is knowledge.

Yet these are just so many myths and legends, of the kind we thought we had left so far behind.

73

These are not welcome insights. The apostles of reason have, after all, been reciting these liturgies for quite time. At some point in that recitation they forgot that these myths and legends were just stories, and in that moment their belief in reason turned to faith. They now wish to say of their reason that '*This* is truth, *this* is knowledge, this and *nothing* else'.

Yet their reason undermines itself. As we will demonstrate, there are no reasonable grounds to think that reason gives us access to an objective reality. Because of this, reason cannot be a reliable guide to truth. Because it is no reliable guide, any truth which it coincidentally stumbles across cannot be considered knowledge. The reasons for this are as follows:

CIRCULARITY

72

The first reason is *circularity*.

An argument is circular when it assumes the truth of its conclusion in its premises. For example:

> James says that he always tells the truth
>
> James always tells the truth
>
> Therefore, James always tells the truth

Circular arguments don't really prove anything. The argument above is essentially 'James always tells the truth because James always tells the truth'. This doesn't tell us anything new. If you weren't already convinced that James always told the truth, this argument would do nothing to convince you to the contrary.

Circular arguments are disdained for other reasons too. After all, if proving a statement were as easy as repeating that same statement as a reason, then you could prove anything and everything, instantly. This would remove the whole point of reasoned argument. Imagine that I could prove that the Earth was flat by saying that it was flat, and that you could prove it to be round by referring to its roundness (and imagine that *both* of us were right at the same time).

So, reason forbids circular arguments. Indeed, circular arguments need to be forbidden if reason is going to be a useful tool. But, importantly for us, how does this prohibition apply to arguments that try to justify reason's own claims to truth?

Take deduction for example. You could try to show, using deductive reasoning from premises to conclusions, that deductive reasoning reaches the truth – that if any premises are true then a conclusion validly reached from those premises is necessarily true as well. What would this accomplish though? The conclusion here would be 'deductive reasoning leads to truth'. But you would have already assumed that conclusion by using deductive reasoning to reach it. And, if you hadn't assumed that, then why would you have used deduction in such an argument? So deduction, if proved using deductive means, isn't proved at all.

Or take induction. You might defend induction by saying that it obviously works, has worked in the past, and so will probably continue to work in the future. On the face of it this seems reasonable. But what are you really saying? After all, inductive reasoning is itself the reasoning from past repeated instances to general rules. The argument above moves from numerous past instances of induction working to a general rule that induction works. So it is an inductive justification for induction. But this is circular – it already assumes that induction reaches truth. If you didn't assume that then you wouldn't have used induction, and that argument wouldn't have been made.

Now take perception. Perception doesn't really deal in arguments as such, but you can imagine trying to confirm the evidence of your senses using your senses. By, say, audibly tapping the computer screen, in order to confirm the evidence of your eyes with that of your fingers and ears. In this way we confirm perception with perception. But what is going on here? If you were trying to verify the accuracy of perception itself, the ability of your senses to communicate objective aspects of the world to you, then using perception to do so would be circular. It would assume the accuracy of perception which was itself at issue. And if you weren't assuming the accuracy of perception, why would you have used it in that verification?

70

Imagine that you try some different approaches though. There's no reason why deduction can only be justified with deductive arguments, or induction only justified with inductive arguments. Instead, you might try to justify deduction using induction – 'But deduction has always worked in the past!' – or through perception – 'Why can't you just see that $((x \to y) \models (\grave{}y \to \grave{}x)?!'$. Or maybe you justify induction using deduction, or perception. Or justify perception using deduction, or induction. And, in fairness, none of these attempts would be directly circular. Nevertheless they fail.

Say that you justify deduction using an inductive argument, as above. Then what is justifying that use of induction? If nothing is, then you cannot rely on that inductive argument to have justified deduction. And, if the use of induction is justified by another inductive argument, then the logic becomes circular. Further, if the use of induction is justified by a deductive argument then all that's been drawn is a bigger circle. Induction was only being used to justify the use of deduction, after all, so providing a deductive argument for it would in effect be using deduction to justify itself. So the only path left is to somehow justify induction using perception. But the same problem arises again. If nothing is justifying that use of perception, then nothing is justifying induction, so nothing is justifying deduction. If that use of perception is justified only by perception, then the argument becomes circular. And If perception is justified by either deduction or induction then we have again drawn only a larger circle.

And so on.

69

You might argue that the list of mental process I've provided is incomplete. You might place intuition or revelation alongside deduction, induction and perception. This would make the task of demonstrating the circularity more complicated. The outcome would however remain unchanged. No matter how many processes of justification there are, each must be justified, or else be arbitrary. And each of those processes must be justified by itself, by nothing, or by a further justifying process. And that further process must in turn be justified by itself, nothing, or another justifying process. And so on, until you run out of justifying processes.

68

What if you decide to allow circularity in your reasoning? That would eliminate these troubling critiques, but at an equally troubling price. As previously discussed, if circular reasoning is allowed then anything can be proven, no matter how absurd or contradictory. At that point reason becomes trivial, as it becomes capable of simultaneously affirming or denying anything and everything.

But what if we just abandon *this* kind of circularity? Say, the kind of circularity that uses a particular reasoning process to justify the accuracy of that very process? For some this will be a tempting route, but it too fails in the end. For one thing, there is no reason for this demarcation beyond convenience, which isn't terribly convincing. For another, this still allows too much, still allows too many absurd examples. There's the hypothetical example of counter-induction – where the fewer past instances there are of a rule being true, the more likely it is that that rule is true. Counter-induction has never worked in the past, of course, and is terrible at predicting future results. But, according to the logic of counter-induction, that 'never having worked in the past' is a very good reason why counter-induction would be true. Accordingly, you can get a circular justification for both induction and counter-induction. This cannot be right though, as they make exactly opposite predictions. But we don't even need our absurd examples to be hypothetical. Many people have an intuition that intuition is the way to truth, a hunch that hunches are correct. Others have revelations that revelation is the source of enlightenment, or have faith that faith will not lead them astray. The evasive maneuvers described above allow *these* processes to justify themselves, to pull themselves up by their bootstraps, just as well as they do the typical processes that constitute reason. And that is a result that our passionate defenders of reason are loathe to permit.

EMPTINESS

The second reason is emptiness.

One of the main justifications we have for our reason is that it gets us closer to an objective reality, that through using deduction, induction and perception we can make some kind of contact with the real. Deduction has no substance to it though – it is merely a way of rearranging information already given. It relies wholly for its content on the premises provided. Induction is just as insubstantial – it is merely a method of distilling certain rules from experience. It depends wholly on those experiences for its content. So then, perception must be the access point of the objective world into reason, and through reason into us. Yet we have no reason to believe that perception is anything of the sort. Reason is empty, and in it the objective reality which we seek is nowhere to be found.

66

Deduction can never tell us anything new, as an argument is valid only when the conclusion must be true if the premises are. Anything in the conclusion that goes beyond what is strictly implied by the premises is invalid. For example:

All humans will die

I am human

Therefore, I will die, within the next 10 years

The first four words of the conclusion are a valid conclusion. They are necessarily implied by the two premises. The last five words of the conclusion are invalid though, as they are not necessarily implied by the two premises.

Deductive reasoning cannot produce new information – it can only rearrange the information that's there already. It is invalid to go any further than that rearrangement, forbidden to make any substantive addition. It is a tool for analysis, not discovery. So the statements that it analyses must come from somewhere else.

That 'somewhere else' is partly induction. Take 'All humans must die'. You likely have many experiences and sense data (whether 1st or 2nd hand) that confirm this rule, and few experiences that contradict it.

By distilling experiences into rules, induction can provide the rules which deduction then applies and interrelates. But induction is just as empty as deduction, as induction requires content to extrapolate from. A rule not derived from content sourced elsewhere – whether deduction, induction, or perception – would be inductively invalid. The rule that 'all humans will die' would not be justified without the content from which that rule is distilled. Insofar as induction reaches beyond that, the rules it distils are invalidly reached. It too requires input from another source. And, as both induction and deduction are empty, that leaves perception as the last source to look to.

65

Perception provides the experiences, without which induction would be empty of content. Induction provides the rules, without which deduction would be empty of content. Everything hinges on the information provided by perception. The question, then, is whether we can trust that information provided by perception as a reliable point of contact with an objective reality.

There are some radical hypotheticals that might rob you of any certainty about that. For example, there is the possibility that this is a dream, or that you are a brain in a vat somewhere, and this is a simulated reality. As Descartes hypothesized – and the Gnostics actually believed – it's also possible that the world you see before you is the product of a deceitful demon. Then there is the possibility of creating computer simulations of life, and those computer simulations then creating simulations of life within that simulation (and so on) until the number of simulations far outnumbers the original objective reality, making it far more likely than not that we live in such a simulation. Further, the characteristics of such a dream, or simulation, or illusion might be such that it would be impossible for us to detect. Perception would then inform us of illusion rather than reality. The experiences extrapolated into rules and subsequently analyzed would be false. And the whole project would wither, poisoned at the root.

But we needn't be so radical. Assume for a moment that you live *in* reality in some fashion. How do you then perceive that reality? Through your eyes, ears, skin, taste buds and nostrils, perhaps with some obscure senses relating to balance and spatial awareness thrown in too. Everything you have ever encountered in this world has been a triangulation of those few sensory properties. Further, that triangulation has been at a certain scale – we cannot engage meaningfully with things that are much larger or much smaller than us. Think of what is left out in this picture. Perhaps imagine a worm, or a bacterium, and the limited world these must experience with their rudimentary senses. Would you say that either of those had a picture of objective reality? Our senses are just as much of a rudimentary snapshot. To others we may be as worms, and those others may be as bacteria to further others, and so on. It feels like the world is complete only because this limited picture is all we have.

And think of what those experiences are. A wandering photon that enters your eye, a ripple of air that strays into your eardrum, some airborne particle that lodges in your nose. Then those are converted by the brain into distinct sensory qualities, combined in some way to form coherent objects, unconsciously screened to avoid overwhelming us with sensory information, fitted into pre-existing senses of space and linear time etc. And with this limited and distorted snapshot you would wish to claim truth? At most, we understand our brain's *representation* of photons, of sound-waves, of olfactory particles, of resistance. But to assume that this is an accurate rendering of a reality that lies beyond those representations is naive.

64

Ultimately, the problem is a simple one. We experience various sense impressions, and treat the conjunction of those impressions as objects that *really* exist. But can we really do this? From where do we get the idea that those sense impressions add up to something more than the sum of their parts? The most we can really say is that we experience those sense impressions. This is uncontroversial – the experience of them is itself proof of their experience. But they are empty of any definite connection with an objective reality.

You have various sense perceptions. Those experiences are generalized into rules. Those rules are combined with other rules, and applied to more perceptions. But 'reality' and 'truth' need never enter this picture. The picture, and life, works perfectly well without them.

ABSTRACTION

63

The third reason is abstraction.

Let's assume that those individual perceptions you experience correspond in some way to an objective reality. That, for argument's sake, they are a fleeting glimpse of the real. What happens after that photon hits your eye and the corresponding electrical pulse hits your brain? You transform that sensory impression into something shadowy, abstract, and altogether different – something far more human even than it was before. So, even if your perceptions convey reality, you have to distort them out of all proportion before anything can be done with them.

62

Take perception. You see a flash of color, hear a dull thud, perhaps smell a light fragrance, and then see a patch of stable red color at your feet. You reach out to touch it and you feel resistance. You pick it up, and biting into it you taste sweetness, mixed with a hint of bitterness.

In speaking of *it*, you've created an object that links these individual perceptions together, an object that is treated as the cause of them in some way. Yet this supposed object can't be experienced apart from those qualities. That there is something that these perceptions reside in, or are caused by, is impossible to verify. You're already abstracting – attributing a common basis for numerous impressions, and labelling this imaginary axis an *object*. You might then also conceive the changes in those sensory impressions as an event occurring to that singular object. Instead of a series of objects appearing and disappearing in a sequence ending at the ground, you see a single object falling. You take the first step away from reality.

Next, you perceive this object as a member of a category of objects. This object is an apple, and the movement is a fall. And you perceive this – no intellectual effort is needed to look at the shape or consult your memories. In most cases, the perception and the classification occur in the one glance.

In identifying this object as an *apple*, you've converted it into a member of a particular category. It no longer exists as an isolated object. But this category called 'apple' doesn't have any real existence either. It is a mental grouping based on the perceived shared characteristics of certain objects. To treat an apple as a really existing thing is to confuse language with reality. You've abstracted again – the object being perceived is now intermingled with a constructed mental category. Further, it is an arbitrary category – we could just as easily (and often just as usefully) group fruits into different labelled categories on the basis of their color, or their size, or their deliciousness. You retreat one step further.

Now let's take induction. You notice that this apple started on the branch, moved at an accelerating pace through the air, then dropped to the ground. You think of other apples. They have exhibited this same movement as well. Perhaps you experiment a little. You pick up the apple, release your grip, and it drops to the ground. You think about these similarities.

In examining apples as a category, the individual objects categorized as apples are now falling even further out of view. The individual nuances of each apple and its fall are now less important than the commonalities between these events. You've moved away from the individual apple, and are now thinking in terms of the category 'apple'. The individual apples now have significance only as part of this mental category, and to the extent that they can teach us lessons that pertain to it. You take another step into the mind.

You notice a regularity in these events occurring to the apples. Without support – from the tree, or your hand – they fall to the ground. You formulate this regularity into a rule – 'If unsupported, an apple will fall to the ground'.

By a mental process the similarities between disparate events have been distilled into a rule, and the differences between them have become irrelevant. Instead of discrete events there are rules, and those events have importance insofar as they support or contradict the rule. You've abstracted again – events involving objects have been replaced with rules governing categories. Reality recedes a little further.

Now take deduction. You apply you rule to an apple – you approach it, pick it off the branch, let it go, and watch it fall neatly to the ground. Success. You move further down the branch, and now come to a helium balloon disguised as an apple. You pick it off the branch, leave it unsupported, and as you expect to see it fall to the ground it floats upwards through the air. Unprecedented. You apply your rule to this experience in an attempt to find a conclusion that clarifies things:

If unsupported, an apple will fall to the ground

This object did not fall to the ground when unsupported

Therefore, this object is not an apple (though, if sufficiently deceived, you might have instead adjusted the rule about unsupported apples falling)

You're now using the rule to determine whether particular objects fit into a certain category. This involves analyzing the interaction between the events involving an object, the attributes of a particular category as expressed in a rule, and the inclusion of an object into a category. You've abstracted again – examining the relationship between different abstracted categories. You are taking that last fateful step.

Through a similar process as before, you've now distilled the rule that 'If an apple falls to the ground, it will bruise'. You suspect that this might have some sort of relation to the previous rule. You want to identify this relationship so that you can avoid spoiling good apples in the future:

If unsupported, an apple will fall to the ground

If an apple falls to the ground, it will bruise

Therefore, if unsupported, an apple will bruise

Now you're applying rules governing categories to other rules governing categories, in order to produce new rules governing categories. You've abstracted again – even objects and events have been subtracted now.

61

You look around, after having taken this last, fateful step. You find yourself in a universe of rules (abstracted from events, abstracted from objects, abstracted from perceptions) and categories (abstracted from members of categories, abstracted from objects, abstracted from perceptions). If you ever *were* in reality, you certainly are no longer. No, this world is one of mental abstraction – human through and through.

This is only the beginning of the abstraction, too. That perception of an apple falling was interrelated and tested and refined until it become a rule about all objects, to a rule about gravity, to a rule about space-time, to, perhaps soon, a theory of everything. We could develop from those deductive interactions a system of pure logic expressed only through symbolic notation, and deliberately isolated from perception. Or we could use these hypothetical examples to illustrate a skeptical argument concerning the mediation of 'the world' through human reason. The list goes on, in ever higher orders of abstraction.

60

But the more abstract your thoughts become, the more they become human. They look less and less like that collection of colors, sounds and smells they once were. This is necessary if we are to think and understand. Those processes of understanding, after all, cannot get a grip on the particular and unique in every moment. That chaos has to be distilled into simple and manipulable concepts; objects, categories, events, rules. But these concepts are not the same as the material from which they are derived. They are simplified, distorted, stretched and twisted. They are humanized.

To understand your experiences you must first falsify them. So, in the end, you understand only your falsifications.

REGRESSION

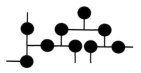

59

The fourth reason is regression.

This is somewhat similar in form to the regress that we outlined in *Good & Bad*, and also shares some similarities with the section on *Circularity*.

Take deduction. Deduction requires premises which, if true, will guarantee the truth of the conclusion. For example:

> If it is raining, the pavement will get wet
>
> It is raining
>
> Therefore, the pavement will get wet

If the two premises are true then the conclusion has to be true as well. But how do you know whether those two premises are true? This is an important question as, if they're false, then your conclusion will be unsound. So how do we go about proving them? Well, if you limit yourself to using deduction to prove them, then those premises must be proved using further premises which lead deductively to your original premises. And maybe you can do so. But, then, the problems have only multiplied. Instead of having 2 statements to prove we now have 4. And we how do we prove those? Again, if we limit ourselves to deduction we'll prove those further premises using further further further premises. But now we have 8 statements to prove! And so on.

This expansion can only end in 3 ways. Firstly, it can end in premises that are taken to be true without being justified by anything else – axioms. We will say more about these soon. Secondly, the regress could end by circling back on itself. This would make the chain circular, so it wouldn't prove anything. Thirdly, the infinite expansion of premises might never end. In that case there would be no justification either.

What does this mean? Conclusion a is justified by premise b, and b by c, then c by d. So if d is unjustified then so is c, and if c then b, and if b then a. The lack of a foundation makes the whole chain collapse.

58

Or take induction. Induction requires experiences, commonalities between which are distilled into rules.

But if the experiences on which you base the rule are unjustified, or untrustworthy, then the rule will be as well. And, if you're only using induction, how will the reliability of those experiences be justified? With another rule justified by experience, of course. But how can the experiences that guarantee this justifying rule be trusted? If they cannot be trusted then neither can that rule doing the justifying. And if that rule cannot be trusted then neither can the experiences from which your original rule was derived. Rule a is justified by experiences a, experiences a by rule b, rule b by experiences b, experiences b by rule c. And so on.

The implications are the same as for deduction. If the chain ends in a rule or experiences that are not justified, then your entire chain becomes unjustified. If the chain is circular or infinite it dissolves.

57

Now take perception. Imagine that you see an apple before you. You want to ensure that this isn't an illusion though. But, at the moment, you can only use perception to do so. What do you do? You might confirm your sight of the apple with touch – you grasp the apple in your hand. Perhaps you feel resistance in the palm of your clenched hand – so far so good. But the thought occurs that your touch may have deceived you – you taste it. You're placated for now but, later, doubts seep in again and you look at the apple once more, using a visual perception to confirm the one you had before.

By now the problem should be clear. If perception a is justified by perception b, then perception b must also be justified if that justification of a is to mean anything. So you justify b with c. But now c is unjustified! And so on.

If the chain ends in faith, becomes circular, or doesn't end at all then as usual the chain dissolves.

56

You could object at this point. What if you used perception or induction to break the deductive regress? Instead of justifying a conclusion in an infinite sequence of premise/conclusion steps, what if you could use a statement produced by perception (e.g. 'it is raining') and/or induction (e.g. 'if it rains, the pavement will get wet'). In that way the reductive regress can be broken.

But this has only doubled our problems. Now 'If it rains, the pavement will get wet' is subject to an inductive regress. And 'It is raining' is subject to a perceptual regress.

Perhaps you object again. The inductive regress can itself be broken – using either perception (trusting the experiences that inform a rule) or deduction (using deduction to justify the rule guaranteeing those experiences). And the perceptual regress can be broken as well! Perhaps you can find a deductive or inductive reason to trust this particular evidence of your senses.

But changing the justifying process in this way only changes the kind of regress you are subject to. Wherever you step, a fall through infinity awaits. And though you can stop yourself falling momentarily, it is always at the cost of beginning to fall again in a different direction.

This is now, in fact, a regress of regresses, a meta-regression if you will. Imagine that you've come to a conclusion using deduction (D). You now have a deductive regress (DR) that you wish to break. To do so you need either perception (P) or induction (I). But using P leads to a perceptive regress (PR), and I to an inductive regress (IR). And PR can only be broken using I or D, which would lead to either IR or DR. And IR can only be broken using P or D, leading to either PR or DR. Any particular regress cannot be broken without instantly creating another. And that regress cannot be broken without creating yet another.

And so on.

55

But surely, you ask, there are some statements whose truth we can accept without further justification. Some solid ground to stop us falling through the air, and from which we might build more securely. Something like 'I am', maybe, or perhaps 'A is A'. We will call these axioms. This route is, understandably, a reasonably popular way of trying to break these regress-style arguments. However, it is as unsuccessful as all the others.

Firstly, if some axioms are acceptable, why can't I just claim any random statement as an axiom? Something like 'the world is flat' or 'I am god'. Is it because there are reasons against accepting such axioms, and reasons in favor of accepting yours? Perhaps. But if there are reasons for accepting some axioms and not others, then neither are really axioms, as their acceptability is dependent on some sort of external reason after all. The regress then restarts, demanding reasons for why your axioms are acceptable but mine are not.

Or maybe you bite the bullet and say that *yes*, any starting point will do, no reasons are required for any chosen axiom. But this too has disturbing consequences. If any individual reasoner's chosen starting point can be accepted as unquestionably true, then from those different starting points we may build in entirely different directions, many of which will eventually contradict each other entirely. This makes reason contradictory. Further, anyone could reach any conclusion they wished to reach, instantly, merely by nominating it as an unquestioned axiom. This makes reason trivial.

Further, if you look back at the axioms that people have treated as unquestionably true in the past – that God exists, for example, or that the clearer and more distinct an idea is the more it must be true – then you'll realize how ridiculous and absurd many of them seem. Any axioms chosen by a thinker say far more about the society they live in, its unquestioned foundations and uninterrogated assumptions, than any real truth. When somebody asserts a truth as unquestionable we may very well ask 'Unquestionable to who?'. Accordingly, there's every reason to suspect that any axiom you wish to rely on will be just as subject to future revision.

54

So if there is an objective reality waiting out there to be discovered, reason isn't going to get us there. The regress means that reason must ultimately collapse into faith – the faith of accepting a statement without reason, the faith of accepting a circular argument, or the faith of accepting something despite the infinite regress.

Accordingly, the conclusions you reach are determined in advance by the axioms you begin with. Reason is merely a way of disguising what you've already taken on faith.

AMBIGUITY

● ○ ○
○ ● ●
○ ●

53

The fifth reason is ambiguity.

This is a critique focused on induction, rather than perception or deduction. It's about the different interpretations and rules that can be derived inductively from perception. That number of explanations turns to ambiguity over whether any particular explanation is true.

Why is this problem with induction important enough to be a problem for reason as a whole though? It's because of the important role that induction plays between perception and deduction. Induction is the process that connects the two – through it the raw material of perception is turned into rules that can be analyzed and applied using deduction.

Without induction there would be no rules to be analyzed. As we have already discussed, deduction is incapable of generating rules by itself, as to generate them from nothing would be an invalid inference. Further, without induction, perception would be a discontinuous series of events, with little rhyme or reason to them. We would have no way of turning that flood of information into meaningful patterns.

Without induction, deduction and perception might run in parallel, each uninformed by the other. Perhaps some pure logic or mathematics would be possible, and perception might still exist as a raw torrent of noise. But reason would not work as it does.

52

So, take induction. You are in a village. There is a drought. You need rain, desperately, or your crops will fail and you'll all starve. So you pray for rain. You all stop work, gather in a circle, hold hands, close your eyes, and pray in unison for it to rain. And a week or so later the heavens open. Next year the same sequence of events plays out.

From this you distill a rule – 'If the village prays for rain, the rains will come'. Yet beneath this simple induction lies an infinity of unexplored alternate explanations.

Firstly, there's the question of what the events *in themselves* stand for. Because what has actually happened here? The village prayed together for rain, and rain followed. But many other things have also occurred beside you all praying together, each one of which has also preceded the rain.

For example, you all ceased working simultaneously. You all gathered together in a circle. You all clasped your hands together. You all said the same words simultaneously. You all closed your eyes simultaneously. *You* were praying. As was the person next to you. As was your neighbor Bob. All of you were *praying*. All of you were praying specifically for *rain*. And so on. There are millions of ways in which the events of those prayer days can be carved up, and an even greater number of permutations of those individual carve-ups.

Now any one of those other interpretations could be inserted into that rule we induced earlier, replacing the 'if the village prays for rain'. You could have 'If we all clasp our hands together, the rains will come'. Or 'If we all say the same words simultaneously, the rains will come'. Or 'If we all clasp our hands together *and* say the same words simultaneously, the rains will come'. The peculiar series of events in the village supports each of these interpretations, and an infinity of others, just as much as 'if the village prays for rain, the rains will come'. And if you're wrong about which explanation is right there could be serious

116

consequences. If the rain is actually triggered purely by Bob praying for rain, and he dies before the next prayer, then you should all just leave while there's still some food available. And if the rain is triggered by *any* communal handholding you may be inundated quite by accident all the time.

Of course, you can attempt to control for these factors. You could use an experimental method, changing the practice of prayer each time. If the rains didn't come after a minute change, that could be isolated as *the* cause. But a huge number of explanations would bear on that experiment as well. Maybe the prayer only works a finite amount of times, and that limit coincided with this particular change. Maybe God frowns upon this heretical attempt to understand His design, and vengefully withholds the rain. Experiments multiply rather than eliminate the ambiguity. Additionally, the infinity of events hiding in a general situation make testing for and eliminating them all impossible.

51

Then there's the question of explanations standing behind the events themselves. An unknown factor may cause both the prayer and the rain.

You'd pray for rain when things were desperate, when your village had gone for longer than usual without rain. But if it's been an unusually long period without rain, then it is statistically more likely that rains will come soon. So both events are associated with a cause behind the scenes – your village prays in an unusually long drought, and unusually long droughts are by definition likely to break sooner rather than later. Or, imagine that the village priest has a cloud seeding machine. Tired of the villagers' lack of religious fervor, the priest causes the rain by firing silver iodide at nearby clouds once the villagers have prayed for it. In this picture, it is the prayer that causes the priest to use the machine, and the machine that causes the rain.

Once again, ignoring this factor behind the scenes may prove deadly. Imagine that the priest has moved away, and the villagers pray the next year. Praying will no longer do any good, and wastes time that would in all likelihood be better spent moving away from subsistence farming.

Once again, you might be able to control for some of these factors by experiment. You could try to pray earlier than usual, to test whether the effect was simply due to prolonged drought, or imprison the priest to eliminate the cloud-seeding machine explanation. But once again, those experiments themselves may be ambiguous. And the amount of experiments needed to dispel all of the possible hidden factors – even if you could imagine all of them – would make the task impossible.

50

The number of explanations of a simple sequence of events is not fixed. The number is effectively infinite, if one considers each possible variation and its relationship to other variations. The world is too complex, and the events which we consider as coherent wholes are capable of being re-described in too many different ways.

Say that a, b, c, and d are followed by e. Do a, b, c and d cumulatively cause e? Is it a by itself? Or b? Or c? Or d? Or a and b? Or a and b and c? Or b and c? Or b and c and d? Or a and b and d? Or a and c and d? Or some unknown variable? Or is it all just coincidence? See how many possibilities arise when there are just abstract letters preceding one another. Imagine how many there would be if you included the actual complexity of events, and the manifold factors hiding behind them.

Because of this infinity of explanations, there is always ambiguity over whether you've learnt the right lesson from experience. Ambiguity over whether you are just the chicken in the farmhouse, who has learnt from all possible experience that when the barn-house door opens that it will be fed. This is a fine and useful induction right up to the night when the farmer opens the door, walks in with axe in hand, and claim *his* dinner. This ambiguity then leaches into deduction, as we use these now-ambiguous rules as premises to reach now-ambiguous conclusions.

FALLIBILITY

49

The sixth reason is fallibility.

This is based on the ever present personal and historical possibility of making fundamental mistakes. Even if an ideal reasoning process would lead us to truth, our human fallibility would prevent us, as humans, from ever reaching that truth in practice.

This fallibility first manifests on a personal level. You and everyone else has made mistakes in perception – seen something that wasn't really there, misheard a sound and so on. Everyone has made mistakes in induction too – generalized a rule from experience that was contradicted later. And everyone has made mistakes in deduction – inferred an invalid conclusion, fallen prey to logical fallacies etc. Even if reasoning processes were hypothetically perfect, they are not self-operative. They must be applied by people, and people make mistakes.

Because of this fallibility, it's always possible for your beliefs to be mistaken. What you believe to be true may in fact be false, because you have made a mistake somewhere.

But let's look at the subjective experience of error. Holding a correct and incorrect belief *feel* the same to the person who holds them. Until you realize your error, in fact, they are indistinguishable.

So for all you know many of the things you believe to be true are false. Further, you cannot tell in advance which beliefs are false and which are true. So not only is there potential for some of your beliefs to be wrong, that potential casts doubt on all of your beliefs.

You might object that there are some beliefs that you obviously hold more confidently than others. That you know how many fingers are on your hand with a greater degree of certainty than the answer to $(6726 + 746) \times (6098 - 31) = ?$. This would isolate the ambiguity to certain areas. But this solution still fails. Firstly, people are often mistaken precisely about that which they feel most certain. So a feeling of certitude should be no comfort. Secondly, this assessment of probability is itself a belief, and is therefore subject to the same sort of fallibility that it seems to present a solution to. And any assessment of *that* assessment is similarly fallible. And so on.

49

Further, there are other people out there in the world. And many of them believe things that are contradictory to your beliefs. In that event, only one of you can be correct. So the existence of others and their opinions guarantees a certain amount of error in the world, either of yourself or of others. And in those cases of contradiction it's likely that both of you will feel equally right, equally justified, equally backed up by experience and logic. So it's difficult to proclaim with any certainty that you are the one who comes out on top when beliefs clash.

Even further, consider your own life and beliefs across time. You probably look back on many of your past beliefs and shake your head, wondering how you could possibly have possibly believed them. Relative to the present, the past seems filled with error and stupidity. But the present will itself become a moment of the past, and if experience is any guide this present will seem full of errors too. Further, that future present will itself become a future past, and seem equally foolish. And so on. This process only stops with death, but if we lived forever it would in all likelihood continue indefinitely.

You may try to solve this problem with the concept of progress – that although there is always error, this error at least decreases over time. But this progress could very well be an illusion. To ourselves we seem to become wiser over time. But that could be merely because change occurs over time, and as a result our current beliefs align more with what we believed 1 year ago than 5 years ago, and more with 5 years ago than 10 years ago. So from the perspective of the present it seems as if there has been a progression towards truth. But it is just as likely to be perspective instead. If as a 20-year-old you could know the progression of your thoughts until you were 80, you could very well perceive life as a constant decrease in knowledge instead. And no-one, least of all your ageing self, has the impartial perspective necessary to tell at which age you were correct. For example, it's reasonably likely that, at some point, I will renounce every last word in this book. But that older me has no greater claim to truth than I. Their greater experience and wisdom will be bought with stubbornness and cowardly compromise, after all, and no-one can know the fairness of that price.

48

All of these fallibilities apply on a broader scale too. You don't come to your beliefs in isolation after all. You're influenced by the beliefs held in your society more generally, in those easy assumptions and obvious answers and repressed questions that you absorb from your social environment. These form an unquestioned background, a horizon of your thought. What you consider to be true is at least to some degree a product of this horizon.

Suffice to say that widely held beliefs are as fallible as the individual beliefs that they influence. And this fallibility will produce some false beliefs, which are at the time indistinguishable from truths to a particular society. The presence of these undiscovered falsehoods casts a cloud of doubt over all of them.

Different societies also often believe different things to each other – things which cannot both be true. This guarantees that at least one of those consensus beliefs is wrong.

The same society changes its beliefs over time. Laugh all you like at the past – the sailors afraid of falling off the edge of the earth, the villagers cautious of the pixies in the wood. But from the perspective of the future, currently held beliefs will be just as laughable. And from the perspective of a further future that future will be a laughing stock too.

The concept of progress cannot help us here either. Are society's beliefs getting more accurate? Impossible to say. Social beliefs of the past become more aligned with current social beliefs the closer your gaze gets to the present. This creates an illusion of historical progress, but could be nothing more than a trick of perspective, nothing more than a product of the way that beliefs change over time.

47

Neither individuals nor societies are omniscient. We make mistakes. And because we are not omniscient, we don't know where our mistakes are. Everything you believe is potentially an error, the source of a future you's embarrassment. Everything society accepts as unquestionable is potentially a mistake, the source of disbelief and laughter for future generations.

Even assuming that reason is perfect, we will never be perfect reasoners. The possibility of mistake haunts our every belief. So we cannot trust reason as a guide – not only for its inability to lead, but for our inability to follow.

Q/A

46

Q - But what are you talking about?! My hand is right here in front of me. If I ask somebody else they will confirm its existence for me. How can you possibly doubt perception?

A - You don't experience an independently existing object in the world called a 'hand'. You perceive certain sights, sounds and textures. These may sometimes confirm each other. But if you doubt perception as a whole then that confirmation is meaningless. It's like testing whether a newspaper is telling you the truth by checking it against another copy of the same newspaper.

Also, this supposed 'someone else', and their confirmation of your perceptions, can also only be experienced by you through your own perceptions – you seeing them, hearing their confirmation etc. If perception as a whole is suspect then so are those perceptions, and the relief gained via the confirmation of others disappears too.

45

Q - Aren't you concerned that this will stifle the development of philosophy and thought in this area, when we should allow it to develop further?

A - See *Good & Bad* §39

44

Q - You realize that society and individuals would collapse if people actually adopted your position, don't you?

A - See *Good & Bad* §40.

43

Q – Does it really matter so much that some belief systems are necessarily circular if they can nonetheless be mutually supportive and coherent?

A - See *Good & Bad* §30.

42

Q - But you said yourself that statements assert truths! If we have no access to truth then how do statements work at all? And if they didn't work then our language wouldn't work. But we *can* in fact use language, so statements must work, so we must have access to truth, so you must be wrong!

A - Language works because we *think* that statements state truths and, as we'll get to soon, it doesn't even really need that. Whether they actually do so is irrelevant so far as the workability of language goes.

41

Q - What on earth do you mean by disputing deduction? If the pavement gets wet when it rains, and it's raining, then the pavement must get wet! If a -> b, and a, then b. This isn't up for debate – it's a matter of definition!

A - But it is a matter up for debate. We're debating it right now, in fact. And if you can only defend it by saying how obvious, trivial, or intuitive it is then you haven't really defended it at all.

40

Q - But God wouldn't let us be deceived like this!?

A - But any reason you would have for believing in God is subject to these critiques too. Invoking God as a way of answering those critiques therefore fails.

Q - If reason cannot be trusted, why have you used it in reaching the conclusion that 'reason cannot be trusted'? If it cannot be trusted, why do you evidently have so much belief in your conclusions?

A - We'll get to this very soon ;-)

38

Q - But you've never proved that our statements can't correspond to an objective reality, only that we can't know whether they ever do so?

A - See *Good & Bad* §36.

37

Q - But the way reason tells us the world should be – that is how the world is! Reason is confirmed by experience at every instant. Deductively reached conclusions necessarily occur, past experience is a very good guide to future events, and things are almost entirely how they appear to us. How can you deny this?

A - Firstly, that is induction, and induction is part of reason, which is itself being questioned. So your point is circular.

But secondly, and more importantly, it is not at all surprising that the world as you experience it and understand it should conform to reason. That is because you perceive and understand it *through* reason.

Imagine you are wearing glasses that give your vision a green tinge. You say that the world is green. A friend tells you that it's just the glasses. You're not convinced. 'Sure' you say, 'the glasses would make things look green. But look! That green tinge is confirmed by everything I can see. Just look around'. Still wearing the glasses, you confirm that everything is indeed green. 'The glasses just reveal the greenness of the world' you say, wrongly.

36

Q - If you doubt that this world is real, why don't you just jump in front of a car?

A - Because I want to avoid the experiences that I imagine might follow, despite not having any faith whatsoever that those experiences reflect an objective reality, or that I have a perfect prediction of what those experiences might be.

THE CAVE

35

You are a prisoner in a cave. You are shackled so that you cannot move. Your head is restrained so you cannot look to either side of you. You cannot stand up, nor walk away, nor look around. You can only look forward, towards a wall. You have been here for as long as you can remember, and know no life but this. Other prisoners to either side of you are chained in the same way.

Behind you is a raised walkway, and behind that a blazing fire. People and objects move past on the raised walkway, casting shadows onto the wall you face. You and the other prisoners take these moving shadows to be the only reality. You talk to each other, playing games to guess the order of the shadows to come.

You get loose somehow. You walk up out of the cave. You turn back and see the objects, and the people, and the fire. You're confused, shocked. You ascend up through a series of tunnels, your eyes slowly adjusting to the growing light.

Eventually you reach the surface. You see objects in the light of the sun. You look around at green grass and flowing water. Eventually you look at the sun itself, the source of both reality and the illumination thereof.

Amazed at what you have discovered, you wish to share it with the other prisoners, and so return down the winding tunnels to the cave. Your eyes are slow to adjust to the light though. You aren't as quick as your former fellows to predict the shadows now. You try to tell them about the walkway, and the fire, and the objects, and the grass and the water and the sun but they don't listen. They don't want to hear the truths you offer. They grow angry at your disturbance, resentful of the superiority they hear in your voice. And if they could, you realize with a shudder, they would try to kill you for interfering with their peaceful existence.

So, tired of threats, you again make the slow ascent out of the cave, and again behold the world before you. Something is wrong though. You notice with a sinking feeling that there is something flickering about the objects, something strangely insubstantial. You reach for an apple in front of you but your hand passes right through it. Eyes widening with a sudden fear you touch the green grass at your feet. While soft to your eyes, to your hand it is rough stone. You run forward and slam into a wall of rock. The sweeping fields in front of you are just a trick of the light. You look up at the sun, that source of all, and it dawns on you that the sun is just another kind of blazing fire. The only exit you see leads down into the part of the cave you left behind. As you look around, at this new part of the cave, a tear rolls down your cheek.

Must this tear be from sadness though?

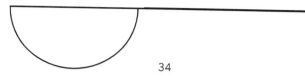

EVERYTHING

34

We have now reached nihilism again, but of a different and more expansive kind. Instead of just rejecting judgements, all of our beliefs are rejected. We have no reason to think that reason leads us to statements that reflect some actual state of affairs in some hypothetical objective reality. The towers of science, philosophy, history that are built on that basis are undermined. Nothing is true.

When I say 'nihilism' in this part I mean this deeper kind, not the nihilism already explored in *Good & Bad*. We could call one of these 'value-nihilism' and the other 'truth-nihilism', or this nihilism 'skepticism', or some other similar demarcation, but there's really no need. You know what I mean.

33

Does this mean we can now say nothing at all? Not even 'We have now reached nihilism again, but of a different and more expansive kind', nor 'We have no reason to think that reason leads us to statements that reflect some actual state of affairs in some hypothetical objective reality' nor even 'nothing is true'?

What then of this book? Does this mean that the reasoning in it dissolves as well? How do we now speak, or think? If we can say things, how? If we can believe things, why? What must we give up to regain the power of speech? And *what* do we say, if nothing is true? How can there be anything left to think after all that has been said so far?

We'll start by examining these dilemmas, analyzing both the threat of silence and the paradox of the liar. Slaying these monsters serves two purposes – it will allow this investigation to continue, but will also force us to clarify the meaning of our nihilism to ourselves. After that, we'll see what consequences this nihilism has more broadly. Then, finally, we'll see if we have any use left for this objective reality we have pursued for so long.

You may find it strange that I'm still using reason, still making statements. Bear with me, and I hope you will find it less strange in another 5000 words or so.

SILENCE

32

Your first reaction to this may be horror. A nightmare image — speech silenced in our throats, thoughts stilled in our minds, the great tower of reason falling in shards towards the ground — is what often springs to people's minds when you say the words 'Nothing is true'. This sort of nihilism supposedly leads to a destruction of communication and knowledge.

This nightmare image may mean that, despite your acceptance of the preceding arguments on an intellectual level, you recoil in horror at the thought of actually acting on them. You may find yourself saying that *because* the consequences of believing it are so terrible, that you categorically refuse to do so, or that it simply cannot be true — inferring is from ought. We've already been through this of course — suffice to say that that move would involve sacrificing your precious reason anyway. In defending reason you would betray it, while I, strangely, would remain true to reason by mounting this current assault against it.

These nightmares come from a belief that knowledge is necessary. That without some idea of truth as our compass we will be lost, adrift. This belief in the necessity of knowledge comes from numerous sources. Some of these sources are intellectual — knowledge is framed as the highest of goods and the greatest of gifts, the only thing of true value. Some of these sources are habitual — we are so used to thinking in terms of this 'knowledge' that it is very difficult to do otherwise. Some of these sources are linguistic — the belief in knowledge and truth is embedded in our language, is assumed in the way we construct the sentences we use to talk to others and ourselves.

Everyone admits that they can be mistaken — that we can think that our beliefs are true when in fact they are false. But it's difficult to comprehend the idea that we can knowingly believe something that we think is false, or untrue, or completely unjustified, or that we can act on ideas yet still not 'believe' them. I know I once had great difficulty with this. If we say that no belief is knowledge, that there is no way of knowing whether it corresponds to an objective reality, we may then think that no thoughts or beliefs are possible at all.

Once again, this is due to the belief that knowledge (or at least *believing* you have knowledge) is necessary. If that is true, and if it's also true that no knowledge is possible and that the external world cannot be reached, then it must be impossible for us to believe, think, or entertain anything at all.

31

There are a few ways this might play out.

Putting two and two together, we might refuse to believe in the existence of anything at all. Refusing to affirm or deny, we check into the nearest Buddhist monastery, psychiatric ward, or couch with a TV in front of it.

Or maybe we believe things in *some* way, but without reason as a way to distinguish some beliefs from others. We go through life believing things almost at random, as if every statement was now of equal weight. We may just accept the things most comfortable for us to believe, skeptical of any other criteria.

Or, perhaps we continue to think and reason in the normal manner, but are torn between that normal manner and the nihilism lurking within. Tormented by anguish and doubt over our every move and thought, we go through life confused and agitated.

Or, possibly, we repress the contradiction between rejecting knowledge and living a life. We either fail to see the contradiction, or relegate it to the darkest recesses of our mind.

Or we are liars and hypocrites, posturing as nihilists while in reality being nothing of the sort.

30

Keep in mind, though, that it is very difficult to actually live your life while not believing/thinking/entertaining any beliefs at all. A completely silent nihilism is more of a bogeyman, useful for scaring people away from questioning the possibility of truth, than it is an actually held belief system.

This doesn't mean that it can't exist in a diluted form though. And, true, we catch some glimpses of it here and there – moments of unbearable confusion about what is really there, a reluctance to form any conclusions in the face of uncertainty, temptations to just throw our hands in the air and give up on evaluating statements at all. We grow increasingly distrustful of supposed facts about the world, more and more suspicious of the authorities we'd trusted for so long. The idea that there is a single truth out there to be discovered, or that we can discover it if there is, is being increasingly undermined. Not coincidentally, this undermining of reason occurs at the very same time that many become ever more zealous with their faith therein.

This sort of disillusionment and bewilderment comes when we view truth as both inaccessible and necessary.

29

This brings us to another reason why this nightmare image is never really actualized – its self-defeating nature. The fundamental problem is that the two beliefs that constitute it – 1) knowledge is impossible, and 2) a belief in one's own knowledge is necessary – are incompatible. If knowledge is impossible, then it's impossible to know that 'a belief in one's own knowledge is necessary'.

If that lack of belief in one's own knowledge truly meant that an idea couldn't be entertained, then 'a belief in one's own knowledge is necessary' could not be entertained, and the various nightmares above would not eventuate.

If, however, 'a belief in one's own knowledge is necessary' *could* be influential on us without a belief in its literal truth, then evidently ideas *can* be entertained without being considered as 'true' or 'known'. But in that case 'a belief in one's own knowledge is necessary' would be false, by the very fact of its own demonstrated influence.

Now, more work is necessary here. Instead of just demonstrating that it isn't necessary to believe in truth to act on ideas, we still need to work out the how and why of doing so as well. But that will come a little bit later, after the next problem we face has been worked through.

CONTRADICTION

The next obstacle that we face is contradiction. This is where we will fail most easily.

Imagine you say that 'all statements are false'. But 'all statements are false' is itself a statement. So if 'all statements are false' is true, then 'all statements are false', as a statement, must itself be false. You cannot assert that all statements are false without also asserting that your assertion thereof is false. This is called the paradox of the liar.

This is quite a large problem for this book, because its conclusions are self-referential in exactly this way. It attacks the truthfulness of statements, and the reason which supposedly guarantees their truth. Yet it uses statements, and argues for them using reason.

The section called *Circularity*, for example, uses a deductive argument in the form of:

A circular argument justifies nothing

Any argument justifying reason is fundamentally circular

Therefore, reason can never be justified

Yet all of those lines are statements. And the transition from the premises to the conclusion is achieved through deductive logic, a form of reason which by our own logic is *circular* and meaningless. Both premises, if not *empty* assertions, must somehow have been derived from inductive rules, which must have been derived from perceptions whose connection with reality we cannot verify. Further, even assuming the truth of our immediate perceptions, once distilled into rules and objects those experiences have become incredibly *abstracted*. Any attempt to justify either of the premises, which must be done if we are to be convinced that the argument is sound, will be subject to infinite *regression*. Each of the premises has to be tied in some way to induction, which infects them with its inherent *ambiguity*. And our *fallible* minds mean that the possibility of error creeps into every deduction, induction, or perception that informs the above argument, multiplying doubt through those long winding steps.

All of those self-reference problems also apply to every sentence written in the paragraph above. And to all of the sentences in this book that precede the paragraph above. And to each sentence in this paragraph, including this one.

You may assume that this dooms us to failure. Imagine you are building a house of cards. You stack cards on top of one another, building the precarious structure layer by layer. After some time and effort, you run out of cards. Yet the uppermost layers must still be built. To complete these layers you will have to take cards from the bottom, destabilizing the foundations, and causing the structure to collapse. You gaze at the structure in annoyance, tempted to destroy the entire thing with a sweep of your hand.

Don't give up though. You can build this house of cards. You just have to construct it in the right way. Likewise, we can complete our nihilism without contradiction so long as we structure our conclusions in a particular manner.

27

Let's start simple. Let's imagine that our conclusion is:

Using reason leads to false statements

'Using reason leads to false statements' is a statement reached using reason

Therefore, 'Using reason leads to false statements' is a false statement

Therefore, using reason leads to non-false statements

Then, after having established that using reason doesn't lead to false statements, we use it to investigate a few of our concerns about objective reality, and end up at the same conclusion – that reason leads to false statements – that brought us to this point.

And so on, in a loop.

26

Let's try another way of saying this. Instead of saying that reason leads us to statements that are false, we'll just say that reason is no justification for a statement. An unjustified statement may still be true coincidentally, of course, but there is no reason to believe it to be so. So:

Reason is no justification for a statement

Only reason is justifying 'Reason is no justification for a statement'

Therefore, 'Reason is no justification for a statement' is unjustified

Therefore, we've no reason to think that reason is no justification for a statement

Well, as we've come to the conclusion that we have no reason to believe that 'reason is no justification for a statement', we use reason to investigate a few of those circularity problems that have been troubling us. Yet once we do so we discover the same disturbing conclusions as before. And so we continue on in another loop.

There are some popular, though flawed, ways of avoiding this sort of contradiction.

You could say, like Phyrro, that you're just entertaining a hypothetical. That you aren't saying 'It is true that reason cannot be trusted', but instead just that 'If reason were to be trusted, then it would tell us that reason cannot be trusted'. In this formulation, you would only be assuming for the sake of argument that reason can be trusted. This fails to overcome the difficulty though – 'If reason were to be trusted, then it would tell us that reason cannot be trusted' is still a statement that asserts a relationship between the truth of one statement and the truth of another, just like 'If it rains, the pavement will get wet'. It is still a statement, just a conditional one. And *any* statement can be rephrased as conditional in some way. To allow this conditional statement to stand as true is to affirm at the same time the ability of all those other statements to be true, and the ability of reason to determine that truth.

Or you could take Wittgenstein's route. When faced with a similar problem as ours, he wrote that one simply had to use the earlier statements like rungs of a ladder, a ladder which must be thrown away after reaching a certain height. It didn't matter that the conclusion contradicted the arguments used to reach it, as once you were at the conclusion those arguments were unnecessary. This argument is not at that point though, not yet. Throwing away the ladder is only possible if you've reached another sort of foundation, or a place where such a foundation is no longer necessary. You can't throw away a ladder that's still bearing your weight.

24

What about another one, like:

All statements about objective reality are unjustified

'All statements about objective reality are unjustified' is a statement about objective reality (our possible knowledge of it)

Therefore, 'All statements about objective reality are unjustified' is unjustified

And so on. We're back in a loop again.

23

I may have lied earlier. There is one radical way around this paradox, a way we might, as it were, throw away the ladder. When told that 'nothing is true' is a contradiction and therefore cannot be true, we could simply deny the law of non-contradiction. It is just another one of reason's commandments, after all, one that cannot itself be justified. The moment you say 'nothing is true' you can break free of the logical strictures that would otherwise bind you. The tower falls in pieces around you, and you walk serenely into the raging storm.

But, while this sort of escape is possible, it is not the path this book will go down right now (partly because doing so would end the book immediately – it is a path on which advice in this form would not be relevant). No, we're going to resolve this contradiction within the framework of reason itself.

22

And, for those purposes, we'll frame our conclusion something like this:

Reason cannot justify our belief that our statements reflect objective reality

Reason leads us to 'Reason cannot justify our belief that our statements reflect objective reality'

> Therefore, we can't know whether 'Reason cannot justify
> our belief that our statements reflect objective reality'
> reflects objective reality

Is this such a big deal though? Does it mean that a
statement is inadmissible, or forbidden, or nonsensical?
Whether this ends in paradox depends, crucially, on the
significance of a statement corresponding or not to
objective reality.

INTERNAL & EXTERNAL

21

Imagine a novel. In it are lines such as 'Bokonon, I learnt from Castle's book, was born in 1891'. This is a statement very much like 'Descartes, I learnt from Russel's book, was born in 1596'.

The first sentence is a line from *Cat's Cradle*, one that describes a fictional narrator's fictional experience of learning a fictional person's birth year from a fictional book written by a fictional author. The sentence is not trying to reflect an objective reality. Yet we can still take it seriously, still admit it into language, still understand it.

The second sentence describes my non-fictional experience of learning a non-fictional person's birth year from a non-fictional book by a non-fictional author. It would normally imply claims to something like objective truth.

Yet what is the real difference between the two examples? If you weren't aware that *Cat's Cradle* is fiction, the two sentences might seem to both be trying to state objective truths. There is nothing in the language used that distinguishes the non-fictional sentence from the fictional one. The only thing separating them is the supposed correspondence of one to a 'real situation' where I learnt a French philosopher's birth-year.

This establishes the narrative voice as one where attempting to correspond to objective reality is not required for language to be meaningful.

Yet reason is not exactly like fictional narrative. Even if we remove the claim to objective truth, this book would be different in important ways to a work of fiction. It is less creative. The techniques used within it are more rigid. The boundaries between correct and incorrect applications of those techniques are more sharply defined. It's bound by relatively strict rules to a greater extent than a work of fiction would be. So while the narrative voice demonstrates the point that statements don't need to assert truths, we need some closer analogies.

20

Imagine a ruler though – a thin piece of wood or metal, covered with notches or lines of different sizes. Some of these represent intervals of 1 centimeter, some of 10 centimeters, some of 1 millimeter. The ruler itself represents the length of 1 meter. These lines occur in a regular and repeating pattern. It is highly likely that if someone else measures a particular object with their ruler, they will receive the same measurement as you. There is also a system in the representations – 10 millimeters are 1 centimeter; 100 centimeters are 1 meter. And there are ways of applying the ruler that do not conform to that system – say if you translated 8 millimeters as 1 centimeter, or read the wrong number of lines when measuring an object's length.

So the ruler gives us a system that is predictable, whose results can be replicated by others, whose different elements confirm one another, and follows clear rules. The ruler is rule bound. So far it is analogous to reason.

But the ruler lacks any sort of correspondence with an objective reality. One can agree that 100 centimeters are in 1 meter. But what is the objective reality of a centimeter, or a meter? Are there real objects that these concepts correspond to? No. The centimeter does not exist outside our collective imagination and use. It is just a way in which we organize our experiences, something that we impose on them from without.

You could maybe say that there are things in the world that correspond to the patterns of lines on the ruler. I could say that the water bottle in front of me is 30 centimeters tall, for example. But this shows only that we're thinking of the world in terms of the ruler, not that the world existed in terms that the ruler now reflects.

So the act of using a ruler is an activity which can be done in a correct or incorrect manner. But this ability to tell correct or incorrect usage is not derived from correspondence with an objective world that might prove us wrong. It instead comes from the accepted rules of using a ruler. These rules are *internal* to the act of using a ruler. They need no *external* support from an objective reality. Applying this terminology, we might say that '100 centimeters are 1 meter' is internally rather than externally justified.

As with the ruler, so with reason. We can never know whether reason leads us to statements that correspond to the 'real' world. But that doesn't mean that there is no rhyme to reason. It is governed by internal rules that dictate whether a statement accords with reason or not. Those internal rules were stated in the section *Nothing*. Whether those rules bear some correspondence to an objective reality can never be known, but that they function as rules which are followed was never in doubt. Reason is governed by an internal logic.

So an argument like 'This glass is full, if a glass is full it is not empty, therefore this glass is not empty' might have no correspondence with an objective reality. You can't prove the deductive logic which underpins it, nor trust the senses that inform it, nor infallibly take these abstractions for reality, nor protect it from the regress, ambiguity, or fallibility. But, despite our inability to justify it externally (with reference to an objective reality), it is possible to show

145

that it is justified internally (with reference to the rules and procedures that underpin reason).

Those rules and procedures cannot be justified externally. But neither can they be demonstrated internally, as reason prohibits circularity, and validation of rules by themselves would be circular. The rules merely exist, and are used. In the same way, it would be nonsensical to ask whether 100 centimeters are *really* 1 meter. That is just how it's defined, and a ruler makes no claim to be justified by anything deeper than that.

Consider a game. There are right and wrong ways to play a game, and those ways are delineated by rules. For example, the bishop in chess moves in diagonal lines. To move it in the way one would move a rook or knight would be incorrect. Yet this rule tells us about chess, not the external world, and that actually existing human bishops are capable of moving horizontally doesn't mean that the rules governing their namesakes on the chess board should be modified.

19

How does this let us escape the problems of contradiction though? We eventually came to phrase our conclusion like this:

Reason cannot justify our belief that our statements reflect objective reality

Reason leads us to 'Reason cannot justify our belief that our statements reflect objective reality'

Therefore, we can't know whether 'Reason cannot justify our belief that our statements reflect objective reality' reflects objective reality

And so on. But this spiral is now no longer vicious. While none of these statements can be justified externally, all of them can be justified internally. Our conclusions may not reflect objective reality, but that's not a fatal flaw.

Of course, everything in the above paragraph is also only internally justified. And likewise for this entire book. It follows certain rules, without ever establishing that those rules are following anything else. It critiques, using those rules themselves, the idea that following them will lead to some correspondence with an 'objective reality'. But it doesn't deny that following the rules will lead to a correspondence with the internal logic of the rules. If made according to reason, statements can have *that* sort of internal justification. The critiques of reason that make up this book also have that internal justification. As does the statement that 'The critiques of reason that make up this book also have that internal justification'.

So by framing internal correspondence (with the procedures of reason) as an alternative to external correspondence (with an objective reality), we can make statements within nihilism. This allows us to articulate our skepticism without contradicting ourselves at every turn, and escape the threatening silence.

Imagine you have a logical argument:

If it rains the pavement will get wet

It's raining

Therefore, the pavement will get wet

'The pavement will get wet' is now internally justified.

''The pavement will get wet' is now internally justified' is also internally justified.

'''The pavement will get wet' is now internally justified' is also internally justified' is justified, again, but also, again, only internally.

And so on.

So we can make this critique without being lost in spirals of contradiction. But to do so we needed an additional concept of correctness. We started out with a rough definition of what we meant by 'truth' – correspondence with an objective reality. We also had an idea of what we meant by 'knowledge' – a belief that was true, and that was reached using a method that reliably reaches truth. This reliable method was taken to be reason so, rephrasing this in our current vocabulary, a belief was knowledge when it had both internal and external justification. This internal justification – which was in essence one of two necessary conditions of knowledge – is now a free-standing requirement for what we'll call 'reasonableness'. Reasonableness is internal justification without external justification.

Reason, without the myth of truth.

18

This does change things though. Now, there's no reason to use reason as a framework, nor reasonableness as a criterion. You can never know whether doing so gives you some sort of privileged insight into the real. It's just one way of organizing things, one of many frameworks you could adopt. There are many others to choose from – religious faith, common sense, intuition, revelation and so on. These choices are not fixed, nor are they mutually exclusive. You can decide to abandon reason now that that lack of external justification is revealed. Or you can continue using it regardless. This is not a decision that can be made for you. This position – of being able to pick and choose frameworks, and act on them despite their missing connection with an objective reality – is what we might call *constructive nihilism*.

17

True & False, and the reasons contained therein, will of course only remain relevant if you make the choice to continue using reason as a framework. If you choose not to do so, then the book ceases to matter.

The same goes for *Good & Bad*. It may have seemed at first that the statements and arguments in that part, as factual statements and reasoned arguments, were refuted in this part. They aren't – they still have an internal justification. You just need to re-read them with that in mind if you decide to continue using reason as a framework. *If* you don't decide to continue using reason then, again, there is no reason to re-read them, because the arguments, and their internal contradiction with this part, become irrelevant.

Likewise, it may also seem that *Good & Bad* is made redundant – if all beliefs are refuted, then, as judgements are beliefs, so are all judgements. You might ask why I would waste so much of our time and energy showing that judgements had no foundation within reason, if they were going to be refuted by the broader application of this part anyway. The reason is this: *if* you decide to use reason, to use it as a framework despite its arbitrariness, then *Good & Bad* contains some guidance as to how internally justified judgements are within that framework (not very). In a similar way, *if* you made the choice at the end of *Good & Bad* to abandon the value of truth, then *True & False* becomes redundant, as the conclusions it arrives at are spoken in a language you wouldn't care to hear. But, if you chose to value reason and truth, then *True and False* provides some guidance about what it is that you've chosen. The two books are nested within one another, and depending on your choices they are either mutually supportive or mutually destructive.

The picture is still incomplete though. After all, reason does not speak with a single voice. This is demonstrated by the critiques in *Regression* and *Ambiguity*.

Regression means that we must all choose a starting point for our reasoning process. That starting point cannot itself be chosen reasonably. Different starting points may yield radically different end results, both of which may be justified internally by reason. Yet these results might be so different that they contradict one another, such that the truth of one implies the falsehood of the other.

Ambiguity means that a variety of different rules can always be distilled from the same pattern of experiences. Each one may be affirmed as internally justified. Yet those different rules may clash dramatically, even to the point of contradiction. The differences in those induced rules may then lead to divergent and contradictory inferences made from those rules using deduction.

This means that there is no pre-ordained list of statements that are reasonable. Indeed, statements which contradict one another can both be internally justified by reason. Yet this should not be surprising. Internal justification isn't reached by matching our statements against a list of statements we know to be true in advance, a list which could be used to eliminate contradictions. Internal justification comes from following rules. It is a method, a technique, a framework. That the same method can be used to reach contradictory results shouldn't surprise us. It would only be a problem if following those rules is meant to bring us into harmony with a singular, objective, contradiction-less reality. As we have now abandoned this goal, contradiction is no problem. The world of reasonable statements is not a single monolithic structure after all, some sort of ethereal castle in the sky whose walkways we explore.

This doesn't imply that reason's insistence on non-contradiction is impossible to follow though, impossible in a way that would undermine the use of contradiction throughout this book. No. For a statement to be reasonable it can't contain a contradiction within the chain of reasons justifying it. But this doesn't mean that different beliefs, all of which are reasonable, cannot contradict one another.

So maybe even the analogy of a ruler was mistaken. Reason is perhaps more like a language than anything else – there are right ways to communicate things, which can be determined by rules you can understand, but no list of correct things to be communicated.

Even this doesn't quite hit the mark though. These metaphors are useful tools, but are no substitute for the center around which they circle. Reason is, in the end, neither narrative nor ruler nor language, but reason.

15

So what use do we now have for the external world, this 'objective reality' that has bewitched us for so long? None. Reason cannot give us knowledge of whether we are accessing that objective reality, nor tell us what it might be, nor even confirm whether it exists. But, ultimately, neither is this objective reality necessary for us to communicate or evaluate ideas. Reason can be used to justify statements internally, without the myth of an external world backing it up, if you so choose.

Objective reality – inaccessible and unnecessary. Humanity has struggled so long and so desperately for it. But we cannot be granted access to it, as we experience the world as humans with human minds and senses. At the same time, we do not need to experience the world from an impartial viewpoint. This is, once again, because we live as humans with human minds and senses. The objective world might exist to correspond with our statements and make them true. But it, and this truth, will never be a part of *our* reality. So, for all intents and purposes, nothing is true. Appearance is the only reality. Or, more accurately, appearance is everything and reality is nothing at all.

14

Many philosophers would now attempt to find some common elements to this intersubjective human reality, some necessary conditions of any human experience or thought, something that could be used in the place now left vacant by the natural laws of the objective world. This sort of transcendental maneuver has been very popular, at least since Kant. I, however, will do nothing of the sort here.

For one thing, I am not confident enough to believe that I could ever discover such shared necessary conditions, that anything I found would be more than a reflection of my own mind or the provincial peculiarities of my own culture. I don't think that anyone has the perspective necessary to survey the infinite variety of human experience, systematize it, and then distill that raging sea into a neat set of necessary and sufficient conditions.

Nor do I have any desire to do so – having dethroned one tyrant, the transcendentalist immediately bows down to another. While I do not judge them for that, it is not an impulse that I share.

SUN & EARTH

Copernicus was the founder of Heliocentrism, a theory which suggested, radically, that the Earth and other planets revolved around the sun, the sun being the center of the universe. This was a difficult theory to argue for – scientific consensus had to be fought, suggestions of heresy overcome, evidence of the senses overturned. But heliocentrism eventually prevailed, and Copernicus accomplished his revolution. In doing so he overturned the older theory of geocentrism, which proposed that the Sun and other planets revolved around the Earth, the Earth being the center of the universe. Both theories were ways of making sense of the pattern of lights that we see in the sky.

The point of this section is not to argue for either geocentrism or heliocentrism in a literal sense. Nor is it to provide a general overview of this particular episode in the history of science. No, what we're concerned with here is the kind of metaphor that each theory provides.

Geocentrism gives us a metaphor where the Earth and humanity are central to the universe. We are that around which all else revolves, for which everything else exists. Our importance is guaranteed by our central position.

Heliocentrism give us a picture where the Earth and humanity are displaced from that position. We are peripheral, a cosmic accident. We can discover what our surroundings are – what we revolve around, what that revolves around and so on. But we discover only what exists in itself, apart from us.

As you may have guessed by now, geocentrism provides a better metaphor for this philosophy. We are all at the center of our own universe, after all. In a more tenuous sense humanity considered as a whole is perhaps a center to itself. But our human minds and concepts permit us no further passage. Things as they are to us will never be those things in themselves. No matter how much we reformulate our concepts, refine our theories and test our evidence, our progress is always circumscribed by this limiting framework. This is the perspective that we are consigned to occupy, and it is up to you whether you greet this consignment with disbelief, despair, or, perhaps, delight.

We have attempted – at great cost and no reward – to depart from this perspective. We have tried to effect a Copernican revolution of the spirit, a heliocentrism of the mind. Such a feat can never be accomplished, nor would we be happier if it were. We should instead learn to love our humanity, our particularity, our stupidity and our innocence.

In metaphor, Copernicus was wrong.

CONSEQUENCES

12

At the start of this book there were hints of grand refutations, transformed existences, powerful nihilism. There were dark allusions to smashing reason's Tower of Babel into splinters, its shards falling like dark glass around us. But now, having done all that, you might think that nothing has changed at all, and could be forgiven for feeling a little cheated. Reason has been forcibly disconnected from any claims to access an external reality. But, as the importance of accessing such an external reality has also been dismissed, this is no longer all that significant. You might imagine that the entire system could proceed along exactly the same lines as it did before, the only difference being the substitution of the word 'true' with 'reasonable'.

This disappointment is understandable, but misplaced. This has, again, been a change in form rather than content. It has not been about changing the beliefs that people accept, nor the methods they use to reach those beliefs. It is mostly about the significance people attach to those methods, and those beliefs. It has been concerned about one method in particular – a synthesis of deduction, induction and perception, which we have referred to as reason. Should we consider this reason as an oracle channeling the wisdom of the gods? Or is it a glass bead game, a beautiful, internally consistent but nonetheless human creation?

You may not be entirely disappointed. Changes in form have an impact that is subtle, but no less powerful for that subtlety. The linkage of reason with truth and a real world beyond our normal grasp has created certain patterns in thought, patterns that persist today. Changing how we think about reason – from providing a justification in knowledge to one of reasonableness – breaks those associations and disrupts those patterns.

11

We'll call the first of these patterns *subordination*. This is the tendency of reason to marginalize other ways of supposedly accessing truth.

Remember that beliefs are true when they correspond to an external reality. And reason is supposedly a way of making sure that one's beliefs actually do correspond to that objective reality. So people believe that reason accesses truth, and that truth is important. Then, slowly but surely, that belief shifts from 'reason accesses truth' to 'only reason accesses truth'. Reason comes to be seen as necessary for truth, rather than merely sufficient. For such zealots, the truthfulness of reason means that other frameworks can only reach truth to the extent that they emulate it. So other frameworks that people have used as their guide – revelation, intuition, faith, less formal lived experience, common sense and so on – are torn down as false idols. And, because access to truth is seen as so important, the supposed untruth of these other methods implies their worthlessness.

Yet these zealots bow to an empty throne. Reason itself reveals to us, in its own way, that reason does not reveal an objective reality. Their tower collapses of its own accord. In fact, their position with truth is even more absurd than that of the religious people they so often mock – holy books never contain verses admitting that the entire holy book has been a lie and that it shouldn't be trusted. Yet the book of reason can be read to contain such verses.

If reason has no claim to truth, then the dominance claimed for it over other possible frameworks collapses. Reason becomes just another way of believing and interpreting, with no supremacy over the others. This isn't to say that any of those other methods really access some objective reality either though. I for one don't think that they do. But they all have a claim to internally justify statements on their own terms and in their own ways. Those other ways are not the subject of this book, but they exist.

According to the Old Testament, the early Israelites worshipped a huge golden cow that they had cast themselves. In doing so they committed idolatry – the worship of false gods, gods that humanity has created rather than been created by. Those zealots of reason should perhaps have read their bible stories more carefully. By worshipping reason, they worship themselves in distorted form.

10

We'll call the second of these patterns *disenchantment*. This is the tendency of reason to delegitimize human endeavors that do not aim at truth.

Truth is associated with what is actually there – an external, objective reality. What is not aiming at truth must then be purely subjective. Things like emotions, myths, narratives, imagination, values – they don't really aim at reaching an objective reality in the same way that truth-focused activities do. They are often mostly subjective, or aim at communicating subjective attitudes rather than objective facts.

Disenchantment makes all of those subjectively oriented facets of our personality and culture fade away into the background. This disenchantment is another consequence of the same belief as before – that reason accesses truth, and truth is what is important. In subordination, the emphasis was on the first element of that statement. In disenchantment, the emphasis is on the second. The belief that 'truth is important' slowly shifts into the belief that 'truth is the most important' or that 'only truth is important'.

Because of this, all those activities that don't aim at truth, or aren't supported by it in some way, come to be seen as unimportant distractions. We spurn our poetry as frivolous, slander our great narratives as children's' stories, warn ourselves against becoming too emotional. We make sure that we are being sensible, reasonable, rational and calculating, not like those fools wasting their life on subjective trivialities. Yet those trivialities, those consciously subjective aspects of our lives, are what makes our lives worth living. They are what stop us from being mere calculating machines, unable to see the worth in the sums we compute. You can demonstrate something rationally, but it takes a subjective attitude to view that something as good or bad, or exciting or entertaining, or meaningful.

This disenchantment has been building for millennia. Philosophers wished to know when we would call a person 'good'. They thought that we would call something good when it performed its unique ability well. They concluded that rationality was the unique ability of humans, so inferred that more rationality was good, and complete rationality best.

This disenchantment is growing further, too. One day, perhaps, all color will be drained from this world.

This disenchantment of the world is again based on the belief that truth is important. The dominant force behind that disenchantment is one particular way of supposedly accessing truth – reason. Yet reason itself tells us that it does nothing of the sort. Indeed, following reason must eventually involve casting aside its claims to truth, realizing that it provides instead only an internal justification. This means denying that truth is important for holding beliefs. The very notion of objective reality withers away as unnecessary.

With this withering away the basis of disenchantment is destroyed as well. Disenchantment, after all, relies on the distinction between a valuable objective world and a relatively valueless subjective world. When reason is exposed as just another element of that subjective world, there is no longer any basis for the elevation of one and the degradation of the other.

9

We'll call the third of these patterns *alienation*. We've already touched on it as a critique of reason, under *Abstraction*. This occurs when people treat concepts as more important than experiences. We've already discussed the processes that constitute abstraction – the distillation of objects from perceptions, events from changes, categories from objects, rules from events, and further combinations and re-combinations of rules with rules and objects. We've already discussed in an oblique way the causes of this abstraction – the use of reason itself, in that reason requires simpler elements than those that perception provides. We've already discussed in some form what abstraction is – taking the world of perception as an imperfect replica of that world of inhuman truth.

This abstraction then results in alienation. Alienation stops us from appreciating the world we perceive, our everyday life. Don't misinterpret this – we should be skeptical about perception, and view it as unreflective of any objective world. But perception is also the basis for so many other parts of our existence – of emotion, of imagination, of intuition, of values. It is, to a degree, the bedrock upon which all our human experiences rest.

Alienation eats away at this bedrock. It treats it as something to be crushed and refined and heated until it becomes diamond. Alienation trains us to live in a world of refined reasonings, of rules and concepts and categories. In doing so, it prevents us from seeing the trees that form the forest.

This alienation is based on the idea that reason accesses truth, and that truth is important. The more refined and abstracted an idea the more it is viewed under the banner of reason, and less under the banner of anything else. That makes it more true, which accordingly makes it more valued. But when the connection between reason and truth is broken, abstraction cannot be truer than raw experience. And when the connection between truth and importance is broken, it would not even matter if the abstraction were truer. In this way, the supremacy of concepts over perception is broken, we are better able to value experience and all that is founded on it, and we can resist alienation.

You can consider the concept of an apple. But you can't taste it, nor smell it. It will not nourish you. For that you need one of the specific instances from which we derive the concept 'apple'. Which is on one hand an apple, yet on the other infinitely less and more.

8

As before, we have used reason (though not exclusively, and not always very consistently) in the critique of reason outlined in this book. Given the critiques just raised, this use of reason may seem self-defeating. Aren't we guilty of all of the above? Haven't we been using the master's tools to try to destroy the master's house? No.

Reason is destructive when it has a particular form. When it claims to lead to truth, or knowledge, *then* it becomes harmful. *Then* it subordinates other ways people have of trying to access the truth. *Then* it disenchants the world of things that are 'merely' subjective. *Then* it alienates us into a world of abstraction.

But if we remove reason's claims to truth then these problems largely disappear. We can instead use reason as a tool, a method of organization, without claiming for it any superiority or domination. The paragraphs above were written in that latter, more gentle form of reason. In the same way, the rest of this book can be re-read in terms of reasonableness rather than truth. This is not just to escape contradiction, as outlined in the previous section. It also prevents this book from becoming part of the problem that it identifies.

Importantly though, please keep in mind that these 'problems' are only problems when viewed through particular values. And they only exist to be categorized as 'problems' when certain things are accepted as reasonable, and only if 'reasonable' is accepted as a reason to hold a particular belief. Again, this critique should not take part in the dogmatism that it criticizes.

THE PRISON

You are in a prison cell, with a glass window fixed high in one of the walls.

You hate this cell, your enclosing prison. You crave the world beyond. While you cannot leave the cell, looking through the window you catch glimpses of the outside world that fill your heart with hope and wonder. You live off these glimpses, craning your neck to see them, mulling for hours to interpret them. They fill you with joy, give purpose to your life and bestow meaning on your days.

You look for longer, think harder. You strain your eyes to see and your mind to interpret. But the harder you think, the longer you look and the more you strain your senses, the more the window tells a different story. It is a hard story to hear.

You are not looking beyond your cell, and the window is not a window. It is a mirror. Through it you look only at yourself, and the cell, in distorted form.

You sink to the floor. It feels like it will swallow you whole. You sit back up, eventually, and look around you once more.

Maybe you refuse to believe that there is no window. You cannot, will not believe that this is all there is. You continue your window-gazing as a respite from the prison, unable to accept the possibility of there being no way to see outside, of, even more unspeakably, there being no 'outside' at all.

Perhaps you break down completely. While you are able to believe it, you cannot live with this it, this cruel joke. The outside world you invested so much is forever closed to you. It is gone, and with it your hope. You sit, despondent, eyes closed.

But, possibly, you might think that a mirror can be just as good as a window. The cell, with its mirror, is the only reality you experience after all – why then reject a different way of looking at it? Besides, without this outside to fixate on you look around at your cell with new eyes, no longer contrasting it with that imagined world beyond. And, as you look longer and think harder, you realize that you were doubly mistaken. As you mistook the mirror for a window, so you mistook your home for a prison.

LOOSE ENDS

6

In an extremely roundabout way, all of this may resolve some of your lingering existential questions. These were mentioned in the introduction and were then promptly sidelined for the rest of the book. We're going to deal with them now.

5

Maybe you're crushed by the insignificance of your life. That in the greater scheme of things (human society, all of human history, the Earth's history, the vast inhuman cosmos, the infinitely vast multiverse of vast inhuman cosmoses and so on) your life is of absolutely no consequence, like a single dot of ink in a book or a single pixel on a computer screen. Sure.

But just remember that these perspectives are ones that we ourselves have constructed. Science, history, and other disciplines make all sorts of claims, but there's no reason to believe they inform you of some sort of objective reality, a reality in whose terms your life *has* to be evaluated. Your own subjective experience is the only world you ever really inhabit, and from *that* perspective your life is not only important but is the sole basis of reality.

So don't feel insignificant.

4

Or maybe you're freaked out about what your own mind is. That your consciousness is unreal in some way. That what you take to be your innermost self is just a series of neurons firing in a complicated but ultimately deterministic pattern. That this explanation leaves little room for free will or consciousness. That what you take to be your identity is really just a story you made up about yourself to link together disconnected experiences and states. That 'you' don't even really exist. Fine.

Perhaps this is all true from some hypothetical objective perspective. But this objective reality in which you do not exist is not a reality that you can experience. You have only your subjective reality, in which I am reasonably confident that you exist, have consciousness, have an identity and so on. It doesn't matter that, viewed objectively, these might be illusions. From the only perspective you have, in the only world you inhabit, those illusions are reality.

So don't worry – you exist.

3

Or maybe you're terrified by the thought that the world you live in isn't the 'real' one. That it's all just a computer simulation. That you are being deceived by an evil demon. That you are just a butterfly, dreaming in vain of being a human. Entirely possible.

It wouldn't matter though. Your intellect is the simulator of your experience. Your perspective is that demon deceiving you. Your mind is what dreams your humanity into existence. That subjective experience is the only world you live in, the only reality worth your time – no matter what computer simulation, evil demon, butterfly's dream, Veil of Maya or objective reality which that experience is nested within. It is *that* in which you must live and *that* which deserves the name 'reality', dream or no. That supposed waking life – objective reality – is the real illusion.

So have no fear.

EVERYTHING
&
NOTHING

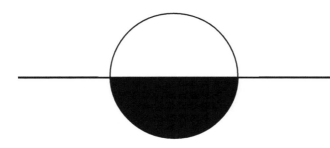

"Before I sought enlightenment, mountains were mountains and rivers were rivers.

While I sought enlightenment, mountains were no longer mountains and rivers were no longer rivers.

After I attained enlightenment, mountains were again mountains and rivers again rivers."

Zen Proverb

So, this journey outwards – to distant realms of thought, through troubling critiques, down paths that collapse beneath our feet – has all along been a journey inwards. All of those words have returned us, in a circle, back to our selves.

You are now the center – you who must decide the frameworks you will use to interpret the world, and the values you will act on within it. And what is this world that you are acting in and interpreting? It is no longer the objective reality of myth, but the subjective reality you have always existed in, a world defined and limited by your own consciousness. In this reality reason is a tool to be used, not a master to be obeyed. This book hopes to bring reason down from the throne we have placed it on, and return you to that rightful place instead.

Yet this book is not like the attitude it hopes to instill. It speaks in statements, and attempts to convince using arguments. The reason that it makes optional is mandatory if you want to follow the book.

This has been hedged and avoided – choices have been given, re-readings urged, fables used, ironic asides included, logical gaps left unaddressed. Yet none of these techniques really address that fundamental tension between content and form. The content tells you to step down from the tower. The form is that tower. In content we have achieved everything, but, in form, nothing.

At the start of this book I said that it could be distilled into 7 words, after all, but it would ideally be reduced even further. A book containing only blank pages would be the most accurate summary of these ideas. Such a book would convince no-one but the truest nihilists though, those who have never heard the word 'nihilism' and would laugh if informed of what it negates. This nameless nihilism is no longer open to us – we who have listened to arguments, examined premises, reached conclusions, tasted the apple, explored the cave and so on and so on and so on. But, nevertheless, it's not too late for us. That is why I am going to stop typing, and why you will soon have to stop reading.

1

I don't know whether the unexamined life is worth living or not, never having lived that way myself. But a life that is only examined is never lived at all.

The important thing is to live.

0

Printed in Great Britain
by Amazon

57751212R00104